THE WOLF IN YOUR BED

How to use writing to recover from emotional abuse

JILL HARRIS

NB.

THE WOLF IN YOUR BED

HOW TO USE WRITING TO RECOVER FROM EMOTIONAL ABUSE

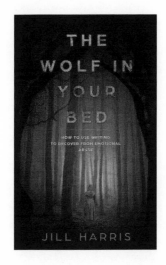

To everyone who has loved deeply.
May you find happiness.
May you come to see the beauty of the gift
you bring to the world.

"Remember, if you ever need a helping hand you'll find one at the end of your arm..."
   (Audrey Hepburn)

   And at the end of my arm I found In my hand
   - a pen.
   (Jill Harris)

- *Have you found a wolf, a narcissist, a person incapable of love in your bed?*
- *Are you looking for a way to recover?*
- *Use creative writing for **personal growth** and **recovery.***
- *Heal your heart with the **DIOL** four stage recovery process:*
- ***Discover** the story pattern of your relationship so you can...*
- ***Imagine** a new ending and a way to...*
- ***Observe** and name your feelings as they grow more positive - until you...*
- ***Love** your life – and find healthy love in the future*

If you'd like to know more about (or receive an advance copy of) Jill's new book, follow this link to subscribe to her newsletter:

http://eepurl.com/dnalCv

INTRODUCTION

"As we stop to consider what is happening to us and what we're made of, the soul ferments, to use an alchemical word..." (Thomas Moore)

"Alchemy: ...the pursuit of the transformation of baser metals into gold..." (Oxford English Dictionary)

The Turning Point

A major turning point in my life happened one freezing afternoon in November. It didn't seem like the sort of day that would begin the most exciting journey of my life. Quite the opposite in fact. Shivering in my study – I was lonely and desperately unhappy in my relationship – and therefore in the rest of my life. I didn't love my self. I didn't love my life and I wasn't living the life I loved because of this.

As usual, I was attempting to escape through work. Busily researching a character for a novel. This particular character was the villain of the piece – the antagonist, the one causing all the trouble in the heroine's life.

For some reason I decided he would be an 'emotionally abusive' man. I didn't really know what the details of this kind of person were. How did he behave? What was emotional abuse anyway? I only had a vague idea. So I did what any motivated writer would do – I googled it.

A few clicks later and there it was. A few helpful checklists to run through. It wouldn't take long. After printing them out I studied them. Apparently – if you answered yes to five or more of them – you were living with an emotionally abusive man. This was helpful stuff

for developing my imaginary character and then, in an instant, my mind flipped.

I wasn't thinking about my heroine or the novel any more. Hard reality was slapping me round the face.

I carried on staring like an idiot at the pages. For a long, long time. Because this was not what I wanted or expected from the afternoon. Because I answered yes to every single question on the checklist.

Me. Not the woman in my book (feisty, brave and extravert – the opposite of my own personality).

Reality reared its wolfish head.

The love of my life was abusing me.

Something dark grabbed a hold of me and squeezed so tight I could hardly breathe. The temperature in the room – already full of icy drafts – seemed to drop way below zero.

A wolf was in my bed. He was in my heart and soul. Love was tearing me up – but the list told me that it wasn't love. Not really. Emotionally abusive men don't do love. This relationship was doomed. I would always fail to please him. I would never be able to fix my marriage. He was the cause of our unhappiness.

It was him.

At first I didn't believe it. I couldn't. Surely this was all wrong. I'd read a lot of spiritual and self-help books. And they'd been sort of holding me together. As I result, I was constantly trying to improve myself. It was my fault our relationship was in trouble. After all, the wolf in my bed kept on telling me this. Over and over again. So it must be true. He was the one who was always right. The list must be wrong.

In fact, I was certain there was something very wrong with me. My husband was making that perfectly clear. For years I'd been trying to be a better person, a better wife, a better lover. I'd read every book I could find on the subject of relationships.

But I kept on failing.

Some days I was a woman who loved too much, other days I came from the wrong planet. Sometimes I just wasn't connected to the Now

or the Tao or the man I loved. I meditated, taped up my mouth, smiled a lot and found a way to agree with him in a win-win kind of a way.

But whatever I did, whatever I tried to do, I was not a better person. If my husband's analysis of me was anything to go by – I was getting crazier by the day. How could I disagree? I was all messed up. Spiritually, emotionally and psychologically bankrupt. My body was wrong, my mind was wrong, my heart was wrong. And I let him down. Without knowing how or why, I disappointed him on every front.

Of course it was my fault he'd been seeing someone else. I just didn't love him properly. That's what he told me. And that's what I believed. So it was devastating to find out that it wasn't my fault. It meant everything to do with my marriage was out of my control.

Frustrated, I went through that damned list again and again. But the same answer kept coming back to me. He was an emotionally abusive man.

My whole world turned upside down and shook me about so hard I could almost feel my teeth rattle. A few months later, I left him.

I still loved him but I couldn't deal with feeling so crazy every day of my life.

Don't get me wrong. We all have to be accountable to ourselves and others for the mistakes we make. It's a good and healthy thing to take responsibility for what your mistakes are - and put them right. But sometimes, and this is probably shocking for some of you to hear, sometimes – *someone else is to blame for your unhappiness*. For many years the advice has been that you choose to be happy. It's as simple as that.

Not so.

Sometimes other people choose to create unhappiness around you.

We owe it to ourselves and our families to discover where our real unhappiness is coming from. To observe our own emotions and stop covering them up. To love the life we live – because only then can we live the life we love.

And sometimes that discovery means we have to change things we don't want to change.

And that's the hardest choice of all.

Your writing has saved you

It took me just over a year to accept that I'd fallen in love with a wolf. All that time I kept writing and writing and writing. It seemed to help. In fact, it helped a lot. It stopped me tipping over the edge – and boy, was I close to the edge. Sleeping and eating properly were distant memories. The relationship left me feeling like a ghost, like the walking dead.

I'd lost everything that mattered to me. The man I loved, my home, the dream of our shared future and my dogs.

There was nothing left to do but write.

Then – being a bit of a geek when it comes to research - I looked into the benefits of writing it all out. And I remembered the stuff they taught us in psychology classes at university. The stuff about stories - and how they capture the way we look at the world. So I picked out the strongest feelings I'd been writing about in my journal – and made them into stories.

Only each time I wrote a new ending – one that satisfied me. Sometimes it was vengeful and sometimes it was forgiving. Often it was wild and thrilling. Occasionally it was peaceful and calm. I didn't hold back on the page. It was important to be creative. And the writing was just for me so I could think, imagine and write anything that came out of the end of my pen.

It took a while to figure out what I was doing, how it worked and why it was helping so much. A wise and wonderful woman – a therapist – explained it to me in the end.

'How have you survived?' she asked. 'I've no idea,' I told her.

'Ah. I'll tell you how,' she leaned forward and looked me straight in the eye, 'it's your writing. **Your writing has saved you.**'

Wow! Really? I'd always thought my writing was a bad habit. A way of avoiding the world and escaping from it – not a way of dealing with it.

Then I had a look at what had happened. First I fell to pieces. Then I put my life back together in a way that suited me – shaped it to fit me. And don't get me wrong – this was not because there was anything special about me. I could see how it might have gone. I might never have recovered my self-confidence. I might never have been able to walk out that front door again and face the world. Because I'm weak-willed, easily distracted and not exactly brave of heart.

But something was guiding me, helping me make good decisions. The kind of healthy, timely decisions I'd never been able to make before.

It wasn't the easy route either. I kept making mistakes and slipping back into agonising sadness, anger and fear. It took courage I didn't know I had. It took enormous focus – and I had precious little of that. My nerves were in million pieces, jangling at every loud noise, every sad song on the radio. In the beginning I could barely follow an episode of my favourite soap on TV – that's how low my levels of concentration were.

But something was there – right beside me - helping me grow. It was like I had some kind of a guardian angel. Only I didn't believe in that sort of thing. I lost my faith in everything when my marriage fell apart.

But the thing was – I'd found something. Something important. And I wanted to share it. So I went back to the writing desk and made a careful study of exactly what it was I'd stumbled upon. And then I broke it down into parts and named those parts...

DIOL: Discover Imagine Observe Love

Basically, through writing, I'd **Discovered** what *'story'* I was trapped inside.

Then I'd **Imagined** a *new ending*.

After that, I carried it on by reading what I'd written and **Observing** how I was feeling – *naming each emotion*. After a while, when these emotions got more positive – I made a note of that too.

Before I realised it – I'd learned to **Love my life** again. Not only that, but after researching the subject of emotional abuse in great depth I felt I could live the life I loved because I knew that:

- It wasn't my fault that I fell in love with an abusive man.
  Abusive men are attracted to women like me. There are a
  lot of women out there who are a magnet for the seven

different types of wolf. Once I understood this basic fact, I realised that abusive relationships weren't my default setting for love. This knowledge set me free from guilt and the fear that I might end up in exactly the same situation again.

- There is a way to spot a wolf right from the start. Because

most abusive men are charming and intensely loving at the beginning of a relationship – it's so easy to fall in love with them. However, you can **Discover** on the first date or two – whether he is likely to be a healthy or unhealthy man to love. This knowledge also set me free. I don't ever need to fear that I'll take a wolf into my bed again.

If I could come back from such a dark and terrifying place; from a time when I could hardly get dressed and walk out of the front door – anybody could. And all it took was a bit of scribbling in a notebook.

An Alchemy of the Mind

It was like an alchemy of the mind. The base metals were all the anxiety, fear, sadness, anger, uncertainty, pain and grief. The gold was

– finding my way to a balanced life – a life full of possibility and hope again. Yes. I was daring to hope. I was noticing the details of life again. I was appreciating each day I was alive in all its complexity. I was loving life.

More importantly, I was enjoying the company of my family and friends again. I was open to them. Instead of being all closed up in myself – I was noticing how they were feeling too. Not absorbing the emotions of others and acting them out. But listening to their fears and worries and able to just be there for them. I wrote all these things down. Observed that I hadn't been able to do these things for such a long time.

It moved me – this ability to connect with others once again. It was humbling and up-lifting. I was so grateful that I was able to love those who were worth loving – through such a simple thing as writing.

That's how this book was born. It's been a long hard road since that awful day in November. Most of the struggle was to find a method to save myself – one that really worked. And then work out why it worked.

My writing had been a way of accessing a part of myself that was nurturing. My inner healer. My **Inner Wise Women**. She gave me something to hold on to. Somewhere to go during those first soul-destroying months of loneliness, pain, guilt and regret. She'll stay with me. She'll never leave – because *she is me*. The wiser, deeper, braver part.

I read everything I could about journaling, diarists past and present as well as the recent research into therapeutic writing.

And then I wrote the book I'd been searching for right at the beginning of my dark journey. It's my gift to you. To every woman who has ever loved a wolf. My only hope is that it helps you to find your way out of that fearful, cold forest of confusion and hurt.

Because trust me – there is a path out of the woods into a new life.

Not just a new life, but a new way of being there for others. Because the more love you have – the more you've got to give. My daughter told me at one point that she was glad to have me back again. I'd been lost in such a painful world that those who I really cared about had lost me too. Writing helped me get back to them. It can help you get back to the people you care about too. And what more, in the end, do any of us want from life?

You can discover that path for yourself. You can imagine a new story of your life. You can observe your growing passion for life as it returns. You can love life again. You can avoid bitterness and yes – even regret over the things that have happened. Finally you'll be able to forgive and let go.

It's a gentle method. I've set it out in this book as a series of sign-posts, prompts and exercises to get you where you want to go. You'll get there in your own time. There are no instant fixes for a broken heart. It isn't a sprint – it's a long walk home. But it will get you there quicker than if you tried to go it alone. I suppose it's just a way of being your own best friend.

A spiritual method?

And I guess it's a spiritual method too. That's for you to decide. What is a spiritual experience anyway? Well, it's not so much about religion. It's about being moved by simple beauty. A child laughing. A cat lying in the sun. A hug from a good friend. It's about knowing that all is well - somehow - in this great chaotic soup we call the universe.

Although there's no religion involved in **DIOL** – it's a way of finding your inner guidance. You could call it a mobile phone number to your soul or your god or your true self or your unconscious mind. In fact, if you want to, you can write prayers to the nature spirits. You can write angry letters to your god. You can call on the muse to touch you when you write – I do.

But it doesn't matter how you use the method– it works with you and with what you believe to be true.

It's a flow - a sort of Taoist way of recovering from trauma. Maybe, if you're reading this book by mistake and the only wolf in your bed is your own fear – it'll help you too. I'm sure it will.

The way it works is as soft as a caress and stronger than a lion. By using it you can - as Oprah Winfrey once put it: *"Turn your wounds into wisdom."*

In fact you can turn your **wounds into feelings, your feelings into words, your words into stories - and your stories into wisdom.**

All you have to do is go in the right direction by**:**

- **Discovering** your story,
- **Imagining** a new ending,
- **Observing** your feelings as they grow more positive and
- **Loving** your life again.

By doing these things you'll be more open to experience. You'll find you can love more deeply the people who are close to you. With one hand you've helped yourself and with your other hand – as Audrey Hepburn said – you're there helping others.

May you do just that. With a pen in your hand.

PART I

Turning wounds into words...and words into wisdom.

CHAPTER 1

EVER FALLEN IN LOVE WITH SOMEONE YOU SHOULDN'T HAVE FALLEN IN LOVE WITH?

"... The poor wife went down and cast herself at his feet all dishevelled and in tears..."

(Blue Beard; Perrault's Fairy Tales)

WHO IS THIS BOOK FOR?

Well, it's for anyone who ever fell in love with someone she shouldn't have fallen in love with. By a stroke of bad luck, she fell in love with a wolf. It's easier than you think. Wolves are addictive or rather – they know how to make you addicted to them. They are arch-manipulators. Emotional abuse can leave the victim hooked, despite the pain. She's experiencing traumatic bonding. More on that later.

And just in case you were wondering:

THIS BOOK IS NOT ANTI-MEN. IT'S PRO-WOMEN.

FOR SO LONG WOMEN HAVE SUFFERED AT THE HANDS OF THE MEN who despise us. Let us set ourselves free of them – so we can give our love to the good ones.

THE WOLVES ARE ALLURING...

Little Red Riding Hood was no fool – not in the original version at least. The wolf was charming, exciting and attentive. He was also a bit wild. Which was alluring at first. Only trouble was – he wanted to eat her.

What do I mean by a wolf? Of course he's a symbolic wolf. Intuitively - we all understand what this symbol means. We know that:

- Real wolves are the ancestors of dogs. They are beautiful creatures full of the vital forces of nature. And as anyone who has ever owned a dog will know – these incredible descendants of wolves are the most loving animal companion you could ever wish for.
- Real wolves are predatory hunters of great appetite and skill. Ever seen a hungry dog eyeing up a chicken? Or a bunch of floppy spaniels chasing after a squirrel? Intense isn't it? Imagine you're on the receiving end of a wolf instead. Treble the aggression, motivation and hunger of your average bull terrier. Then think about how the poor squirrel/chicken/ antelope feels.
- Therefore, when we talk about wolves in human form we're really talking about hunters. **Only these ones are hungry for sex, power and domination**. Control freaks, sex addicts, narcissists – call them what you like. In other words they've got all the bad qualities of a real wolf without the excuse of being a wild animal.

With that one cleared up – let's have a look at the statistics, and find out a bit about traumatic bonding...

THE MALE OF THE SPECIES IS, IN FACT, DEADLIER THAN THE Female...

You might have heard the song *The Female of the species is Deadlier than the Male*. Of course this is true when it comes to black widow spiders and praying mantises. On the other hand – when it comes to human beings, it doesn't have quite the same ring of truth. The statistics below are from a UK government website. It's interesting to note that although this is a massive problem – how often do you hear people talking about it?

Not much.

It's as though we're afraid to mention it.

Ashamed perhaps to talk about the way some men treat their women. It's as though, as a core cultural belief - we still think that men 'own' women and therefore can do what they like with them. The many, many good men out there are not the subject of this book. But that doesn't mean the wolves should be ignored.

THINK ABOUT THIS:

- In the UK **two** women a week are murdered by a partner or ex- partner.
- More than **one in five** women in the UK has experienced domestic violence.
- And it affects more than 25 million American women.
- According to the Violence Policy Centre's report for 2015 titled: '*When Men Murder Women*', **1,686 American women were murdered by an intimate partner.**
- That's an average of three women every day.
- These statistics are echoed the world over.
- **All violent men are emotionally abusive.**
- Many more men are emotionally abusive without being physically violent.
- The scars of emotional abuse **take longer** to heal than the physical ones.

Although emotional abuse can't kill you – depression can. Emotional abuse can cause anxiety-related depression which can cause feelings of hopelessness, helplessness and thoughts of suicide... and thoughts of suicide often, sadly, become acts of self-harm.

CHAPTER 2
TRAUMATIC BONDING

"...an abusive man works like a magician. His tricks rely on getting you to look off in the wrong direction." *Lundy Bancroft*

THE LOVE YOU FEEL IS REAL. BUT HIS IS NOT. LET ME REPEAT THAT – **his love is not real.**

A wolf is not capable of real love. An emotionally abusive man uses manipulative mind games to gain power and control in a relationship. Over time, his repeated acts of love are followed by repeated cruelty. After a while, he doesn't have to bother much with the acts of love. He's trapped you in a psychological condition called traumatic bonding.

Ever heard of Stockholm Syndrome? If you have – you'll know the term comes from a hostage situation that happened in Stockholm in 1973. The kidnappers used mental and physical cruelty to control their captives. They also handed out small, infrequent acts of kindness. After only five days, the victims had bonded with their captors. One woman hostage later married one of her kidnappers.

Put simply, traumatic bonding is a survival strategy. It happens to abused children, victims of domestic violence (both physical and emotional), prisoners of war etc.

Love is a drug or so they say, and it feels good to be adored. It's easy to get hooked.

This is how it is at the beginning: Adoration with a capital A. He adores you. He needs you. You are 'The One'. Then it starts - the cycle of addiction, the cycle of abuse.

THE CYCLE OF ABUSE

The cycle of abuse is always there – right from the beginning. But it's hard to see it if you don't know what you're looking for. In the last chapter of this book I'll show you how to spot the early warning signs so you never have to take a wolf into your bed again.

This is what the cycle of abuse looks like:

- He loves you like no other man ever has,
- he showers you with affection then,
- he's angry and abusive but then -
- he loves you and you know...
- he's controlling - but after a bit,
- he loves you again – but then
- he degrades you
- but it's okay because soon after that,
- he loves you again – so you forgive him
- and so on...

THE SIMPLE ACT OF PICKING UP A PEN

Why is all this still happening in the twenty-first century? Women were still being sold at country fairs in the early twentieth century – but we're well past all that aren't we?

Is it because women are so difficult? Do we deserve to be controlled and dominated because we are so flawed? Is it for the woman's own good? Or is it men? Testosterone? Culture? Nature? Nurture? A combination of all the above? Will it ever stop?

Who knows.

It just is what it is. We all seem to accept it. This book is not about changing male behaviour or getting angry about it. The statistics are there for anyone to see. It's just a fact of life. Like summer rain or wasps in your jam.

This book is about finding the helping hand on the end of your own arm.

It's about the **process of recovering from emotional abuse by the simple act of picking up a pen.**

Remember – women are emotionally abusive too – but in a different way. It doesn't cause the same amount of harm. We'll have a look at the differences between male and female methods of abuse later.

And of course – the main point of this book is to write your way home.

You can recover your joy and one way of doing that is by using the **DIOL** technique.

But it takes work. You have to do the writing.

There are no quick fixes when it comes to heartbreak or deep emotional scars. It takes time to recover from emotional abuse.

But you can do a great deal to ease the process along simply by using powerful therapeutic writing techniques.

PICK UP A PEN AND USE THE POWER OF WRITING TO:

Discover your story→ Imagine a New ending→ Observe your feelings→ Love your Life.

But for now, we'll start off with the facts of the matter in hand. The male of the (human) species can be a wolf. And if he gets into your bed and worse still - inside your heart, he can cause havoc.

THERE ARE PLENTY OF WONDERFUL MEN OUT THERE...

Here's a thing. In the seventies there was a wave of anger about the way a lot of men behaved towards women.

Women raised their consciousness. They looked beyond the fairy tale and were appalled. They saw a huge number of men bullying, raping and attacking women as if it was okay. Naturally, they pointed out that it was not okay.

These radical ideas spread like butter on hot toast causing all sorts of problems.

Men were perturbed.

They were upset because many of them were not cruel or abusive.

Women were also perturbed.

They were angry with other women. What was wrong with beauty contests? After all, men couldn't help being strong, forceful, lusty and daring. Isn't that why we love them? Who wants a man in a kitchen – he'll only get in the way?

And if a woman has to take a few knocks then it's the price she pays for love. Everything has a price, after all.

A lot of women told other women to know their place and stop making such a fuss.

The image of the 'uppity' woman came into being.

She wore dungarees and no make-up. She had opinions. It was a cliché and a stereotype was born.

It caused mayhem. I know. I lived through those days and the sex war was out and proud and arguing in every pub, café, street corner and student flat-share.

INEVITABLY, THERE WAS A BACKLASH. WOMEN WHO TALKED ABOUT this stuff were seen as man-hating psychos. Often they were depicted as too ugly or selfish or crazy to get a man for themselves.

The result? A hush fell over the land.

It was like the three good fairies from Sleeping Beauty had decided that no one was ready for the truth and so they put everybody to sleep. We're only just waking up from that so it's still hard to talk about this problem. So, let me just say this.

THERE ARE PLENTY OF WONDERFUL MEN OUT THERE.

Yup. There are loads of guys who can give sweet, meaningful love to a woman they respect. And they are still real men to boot.

So if you want a psychotic rant against men you'll have to buy another book.

But I am not going to pull any punches either.

There are still a lot of men out there getting away with extensive bullying and emotional abuse towards the women who love them.

It strikes me that these men – or their fathers and grandfathers - were the ones who hated feminists so much in the early days.

A misogynistic, bullying, emotionally abusive man learns this behaviour from his father.

There was a time [this opinion is still held in some parts of the world] when people thought women had only themselves to blame if they were desperately unhappy in their marriage. Or raped. Or killed – presumably.

The opinions of misogynistic men were taken seriously even up until quite recently in many of the so-called advanced societies. They didn't like women they couldn't control. So they made them feel ugly, stupid and unlovable.

Hmm. The times they are a-changing. Thank goodness.

THE PATH OF LOVE IS ALWAYS A BIT BUMPY...

"I have spread my dreams under your feet,
  Tread softly because you tread on my dreams..."
  W B Yeats

Love's path is always a bumpy ride – however well suited and devoted you are. Love can go wrong for so many reasons.

Healthy love means that both partners ride out the bad times together. They grow closer, stronger through experiencing the good as well as the bad together.

They argue – but it's okay. They sort it out and move forward.

Their love deepens. That's why it's worth it. That's the point of being together.

UNHEALTHY LOVE IS DIFFERENT. YOU DON'T GROW. YOU SHRINK. Bad love is toxic to your whole system.

Mind, body and spirit are shrivelled up like grapes in the hot sun if you are being bullied by the one you love.

And the more you try to please him, the harder it gets.

In the end, you find yourself sick at heart.

If you've been in an emotionally abusive relationship for many years – you may well have physical or mental health issues to deal with too – as a direct result of the relationship.

- Toxic love makes you neglect your physical needs. You're too busy looking at him.
- You forget to take of your emotional needs. Too busy trying to second guess what he wants next.
- Your spiritual needs are also unmet. How could you love yourself or the world if you're always on your knees hoping for crumbs of love from him?
- You lose respect for yourself. If he doesn't respect you then why should you?

This book is about how to recover from this kind of toxic love.

Remember: the pen is *totally* mightier than the sword. Using the simple process of writing through the **DIOL – Discover Imagine Observe Love** method of recovery; you too can find a new way of being, a new life.

One that's much better than life with a wolf could ever be.

THE POWER STRUGGLE

In all unhealthy relationships, there is one big problem.

A power struggle.

Power over others is intoxicating and can easily get out of control.

That's why I've said this book is for those who are recovering from *toxic* love. In healthy relationships power struggles are resolved. In unhealthy ones they never are.

Controlling men are addicted to power.

And they are more likely to use fear to exert this power.

We'll have a look later at the different ways men and women are emotionally abusive and why the effects on women are generally much worse.

One of the symptoms often found in victims of emotional abuse is a sense of '*not knowing who I am any more...*'.

They feel broken, empty.

This is because they've tried so hard to become the person their wolf lover/partner/husband wanted them.

They are lost in the woods.

They are trapped in the middle of his story about who they are; his world-view of women.

And it isn't very complimentary. They end up seeing themselves through his eyes. Their self-respect shatters. In this book I'll use the term 'wolf' to refer to an abusive man.

A wolf will cast you into his own fairy tale world – but not in a good way.

In this book you'll discover the story that mirrors your experiences of living in this nightmare world.

CHAPTER 3
WRITING FOR RECOVERY

"Writing is a form of therapy; sometimes I wonder how all those who do not write, compose or paint can manage to escape the madness, melancholia, the panic and fear which is inherent in a human situation." *Graham Greene*

WRITING IS A VERY POWERFUL TOOL FOR RECOVERY.

Only recently have researchers begun to realise what an amazing and simple activity it is for those struggling with anxiety, depression and stress.

You don't have to be good at it.

You don't even have to like writing that much!

A small amount of short writing exercises can make a difference to how you feel, how well you're coping and even your levels of killer white cells.

In other words, writing it out can bring you back to a **healthy state of mind and body** quicker than almost anything.

And it's free.

Using the latest research on writing for health – I've designed a system anyone can use.

Think of writing through the **DIOL** method as a toolkit for fixing the heart − for finding a way towards healthy loving. For recovering from traumatic bonding, toxic love − and finding your way home to the ones who deserve your love.

We're going on a journey together.

A journey through the dark forest towards the light.

In one hand you have a pen, in another a notebook.

Try as much as possible to write with a pen on paper. A computer is okay as a writing tool. But for therapeutic writing, a pen in your hand is like a direct line from the heart, down your arm and onto the page.

And remember. You can always burn whatever you write later if you want to.

You can rip up paper, throw the pieces in the air and watch the rain turn the ink into rivers.

No one else needs to ever see what you've imagined.

The path out of the forest is a steep one.

It's not an easy climb.

I'm not promising instant harmony in your soul and the healing of all your wounds.

Emotional abuse is a tough thing to get through and I'm not going to pretend it's anything else.

However, if you use this book − as well as any other help − such as a therapist, good friend, parent, doctor or priest − I can promise you this.

It's doable.

- You only have to keep reading this book.
- Do any checklists and questionnaires
- Absorb the information about wolves and their stories
- And Write. Yes, write. Write your heart out. Write in your notebook. Write in your head. Write and cry and laugh and rewrite.
- Imagine new outcomes for you and your family, your true friends and those that matter.
- Write your way back to love.

CHAPTER 4
HOW TO USE THIS BOOK

"Everything you do has a quality - which comes back to you in some way." *Rumi*

READING AND WRITING. THAT'S IT.

The reading bit comes first.

It's probably best if you read this book right through first. Then you'll have a good view of what it's about and how to use the recovery tools.

After that, go back to the start and begin the writing exercises.

If all this sounds like too much work – think of it like this. It took years of emotional abuse to bring you to this point. You've been kidnapped and taken to a world where everything you do, say and think is wrong.

That's his world, his fairy tale – and his view of you.

You won't undo all this with a quick read or a half-hour chat with a therapist.

But if you put in the time to take it slowly – you'll reap the rewards. You'll find your way home – back to the life you love.

You'll write your way there. And it's fun.

Creative writing is an enjoyable activity.

Rest assured, you'll never write anything you can't handle. You can only gain from taking it slow, reading to the end – and then starting to write...

Writing Your Way Home

You don't have to write every day unless you want to. You might only have half an hour a couple of times a week for your **DIOL** work. Never mind.

You'll still get more out of it than you put in.

You'll re-discover your self-respect, your scattered self-love. Your ability to love the people who deserve your love.

You'll end up loving the life you live. And living the life you love. In other words, your family and friends will get you back.

You'll be able to take positive steps forward in your career – even if it means a career change.

Your life will blossom fully.

In the end - what else matters?

The writing exercises are simple – deceptively simple, and they build on one another.

It doesn't matter if you haven't done any creative writing since school.

It doesn't matter if you're dyslexic. If you are – you might want to use an audio device to record your freewriting exercises.

Anyone can write freely.

Here's how:

- Just put the pen on the page and write until your time is up.
- Don't stop.
- Don't think.
- Let your pen go,
- Let your hand go,

- Let it all fly out of you.
- Don't edit or think or try and write 'nicely'.

It's helpful to approach it as a kind of writing meditation.

ONCE YOU'VE READ THE BOOK THROUGH FIRST – BUY A NICE notebook, find a pen you like – and write your way home.

Do the Quick Writes one at a time and in the order they are laid out.

They build up – one on top of the other like bricks to build a strong house.

The foundation is reading the book and understanding the different wolves, how they work and how they've trapped you into their Fairy Nightmare.

You'll **Discover** your story – in other words - which unhealthy love pattern your wolf has forced you into.

You'll **Imagine** a new ending to this story – one where you come out of it well.

You'll learn how to **Observe**, name and reclaim your own emotions.

And by the end of it – you'll **Love** your life.

And don't forget to do the...

Quick Writes:

You'll find quick writing prompts along the way.

You can do them all or just a few or read the book right through and then do them later.

Now, if you're ready – you can start right away.

Grab a notebook and a pen and start with this:

QUICK WRITE

Write the words:

'Today I feel...'

...at the top of the page.

Set a timer for five minutes.

Write for five minutes non-stop even if you think you're writing rubbish.

In fact, try not to think.

Just write.

Even if you don't know what you feel. Just write 'I don't know what I feel' over and over until the time is up.

This is a powerful exercise so don't skip it.

THIS IS CALLED FREEWRITING.

It's incredibly good for you.

A bit like vitamins for your soul. And it's easy.

You don't have to be Jane Austen to do it.

No one else ever needs to read it. It's your direct line to your soul/unconscious mind/real self.

And **you'll never write anything you aren't ready to hear.**

If you've been in an abusive relationship you've probably lost touch with how you really feel. This is because your emotions weren't important. His were.

This book will help you understand how to recognise, name and own your emotions once again.

Own them? Well, yes. You have a right to all your feelings. They belong to you and you alone.

And if you haven't already - next time you go shopping find a notebook you like and a nice pen.

Keep them with you.

A lot of writers think hand-writing is a bit more of a direct line to the unconscious. I tend to agree but if you want to use the computer or dictate into your phone, go ahead. The most important thing is to get the words down.

QUICK WRITE

Write this statement at the top of a new page:

In the core of my being right now, all is being healed.

Set a timer for 5 minutes.

Write as if you believe the statement to be true.

What is there to heal within you?

Write about coming home to your soul.

Write about finding your way back to the person you were meant to be.

Write about reclaiming your heart.

THE NEXT QUESTION WE NEED TO ANSWER IN DEPTH BEFORE WE GO on is:

What is toxic love?

CHAPTER 5
WHAT IS TOXIC LOVE?

"Toxic people attach themselves like cinder blocks tied to your ankles, and then invite you for a swim in their poisoned waters." *John Mark Green*

TOXIC LOVE IS A SLOW POISON.

A loving, healthy relationship can lead to a longer, healthier more fulfilling life.

Toxic love does the opposite.

The wolf you fell in love with is almost certainly capable of being charming. Most of them are. All his friends might think he's cool.

He might be successful at work, a fun guy at parties and able to make a great show of being a great dad with the kids.

However, you know there's a shadow over your relationship. You probably blame yourself. But there is something terribly wrong.

His 'love' will drain you.

He's like a vampire sucking your life force. But you can do something about this – you can...

Take control of your Story:

Every life is a story – or more accurately – a collection of linked short stories.

It's a journey between birth and death with all the highs and lows and ordinary days.

In a toxic love relationship your story is hijacked.

The wolf doesn't see you for who you are.

He will have told you over and over again that you are the cause of all the pain.

Don't believe it.

A wolf will see you according to his recurring unhealthy patterns. He'll make you live out his nightmare fairy story. It's a lose-lose situation for you.

You might already have ended the relationship, in which case you will most likely be burned out and hurting. This book will help you process your experiences and feelings through taking control of your story on the page.

And whether you're with him or not - you might still be in love with him. They're easy to love and we'll see why later. But whether he's in your bed right now or you're recovering from a toxic relationship with him (remember, wolves are only capable of toxic relationships, they can't experience real love), **you can still take back control of your life, your story**.

But if he's so loving sometimes - he can't be a wolf – can he?

WOLVES CAN NEVER LOVE

Sadly, it's true.

He's not able to feel love.

Not like most of us anyway. Wolves can never love their female partners because they despise women in general.

It's like a hard-wiring problem.

So don't worry for his sake, **you didn't fail him.**

You never stood a chance at making that relationship work.

Most of us non-wolves are good at love. Too good sometimes. But that doesn't mean we have to keep on paying the price.

WHEN YOU LOVE SOMEONE WHO:

- destroys your confidence,
- drives a wedge between you and the people who care about you,
- makes you mistrust your own judgement, your thoughts, your beliefs

Then that's toxic love.

Love shouldn't hurt all the time.

If you've loved a wolf you know what I mean. Even in the good times you're afraid.

Afraid because you know, sooner or later you'll get it wrong again and upset him.

ALSO, IF YOU ARE

- constantly obsessed with the details of your relationship with him,
- blaming yourself for making him unhappy,
- trying to figure out how to make it work and failing every time Then watch out, it's almost certainly toxic love.

Wolves as I said, don't do love.

This is because they want an ideal woman.

A perfect woman.

Are you perfect? Thought not. None of us are.

But what about female abusers? Haven't you found yourself behaving badly too? Haven't you said terrible things during one of those arguments with him?

Yes, almost certainly, but the thing is...

MEN AND WOMEN ABUSE IN DIFFERENT WAYS

Remember those power struggles? Those arguments over stupid

things that made you feel terrible, guilty and sick at heart? The ones where you felt like you were going crazy? Well you weren't.

That's just how a wolf makes you feel.

Why? Because he's not what he seems.

Remember the wolf in Red Riding Hood's bed? He was pretending to be granny. He even dressed up in her clothes. In the original version all he wants is for Little Red to take off her clothes and get into bed with him.

As I said earlier, power struggles are common in relationships. Especially in the early part – you know the phase?

It comes just after the initial rush of love and right before you really know each other well and have settled into your long-term love groove.

We all tussle with our partner psychologically in some way, shape or form.

In a healthy relationship we draw the lines, learn to understand each other and grow closer through this phase. Boundaries are respected.

WOLVES DO NOT RESPECT YOUR BOUNDARIES.

In an unhealthy relationship there is an endless dance of suffering.

And the longer it lasts the worse it gets. The truth is that over time he finds it harder and harder to hold back his distaste for you – for women in general – but it focuses on you.

It's nothing personal. As I said, he's looking for a perfect fairy princess and you are – well, a grown woman with all the usual imperfections.

BUT WOMEN CAN BE EMOTIONALLY ABUSIVE TOO – CAN'T THEY?

Of course they can.

It's just that in general, men and women abuse in different ways.

In fact, research has shown that women are equally as likely to use emotionally abusive tactics in relationships. It happens across age groups, cultures, classes and religions; in same-sex as well as hetero-sexual relationships.

But – and it's a big but - there's an important difference in behaviour when it comes to gender.

WOMEN USE SHAME.

They let their partner know that he's rubbish at washing up or getting up or looking after the kids or working hard. This does not cause long-term damage because it's usually brushed off.

MEN USE FEAR AS A WAY OF CONTROLLING WOMEN.

Fear is a much more powerful and harmful emotion to deal with.

QUICK WRITE:

Set the timer for five minutes. Write the words:
'*I'm afraid of...*' at the top of the page.
Some writers write to discover what they really think.
Others write to uncover what they really feel.
All of us need to know what we feel whether we think of ourselves
as writers or not.
The point is that writing can give us this gift. For free.

READ BACK OVER WHATEVER YOU'VE JUST WRITTEN.

Have you become more fearful since you took a wolf into your bed?

Most women who are being emotionally abused develop a lot of fears and phobias.

Some of us find we can write a shockingly long list of new things we're afraid of. Fears that were never there before the wolf slid between our sheets.

If you're afraid of things you never used to worry about – it's okay.

Writing it out helps. You'll find a part of your emotional self, a wound, and give it a name.

It's okay.

You'll never write anything unless you're ready to hear it. Your unconscious mind is taking care of you.

Oh, and you might be wondering...

CHAPTER 6

WHY IS FEAR SUCH A BIG PROBLEM?

"No passion so effectually robs the mind of all its powers of acting and reasoning as fear."

Edmund Burke

HERE'S THE SCIENCE BIT:

Emotional abuse induces fear-based anxiety.

This is because a part of the brain that reacts to danger has been over-stimulated.

Every time he calls you a foul name, or criticises you for not doing something he wanted you to do, or shouts at you for doing something he didn't want you to do, or threatens to leave etc. – your fight or flight system has been alerted.

Imagine alarm bells ringing in your head all day and all night.

It would drive anyone crazy.

And even when it stops – you know it'll start up again sometime soon. But you don't know when.

You stay on high alert.

The red light is blinking in the back of your mind. Adrenaline is released. You can't run and you can't fight.

So you run from your own emotions and you fight with yourself.

It's like being in a constant state of panic.

Basically, an over-stimulation of this part of our mental processing is much greater than any other form of emotional pain.

So, if we live in constant fear of harm, of rejection, of losing our home, our friends or children; fear of isolation and deprivation - this has enormous, long-lasting and wide-ranging consequences on mental health.

After a while - you can't turn it off.

Your adrenaline is pumping most of the time. Your adrenal glands are overstretched.

In the end, you're jumping at your own shadow.

This causes major generalised anxiety. You're worried and irritable about everything and nothing.

There is some evidence that an over-production of adrenaline can be factor in the onset of dementia. But don't worry. By using writing to:

Discover your story→ Imagine a New ending→ Observe your feelings→ Love your Life.

You can slow this process down.

You can stop the fear.

You can recover.

THERE'S A PATTERN...

Yes. There's a predictable pattern when it comes to emotional abuse.

Everything is extremely rosy in the garden of love to begin with.

He sweeps you off your toes.

But once the abuse sets in − oh so slowly at first - it takes the form of mind games, verbal and non-verbal abuse which leave you with a sense of:

- self-loathing,

- emptiness,
- detachment from others you care about,
- loneliness,
- low self-worth,
- low or zero self-confidence
- anxiety and/or depression
- helpless desperation.

Add to this the fact that different forms of sexual coercion are often involved.

From this you can see why this kind of behaviour often causes such deep and lasting emotional wounds.

In fact, fear-based abuse can damage your health to the extent that it is a major cause of emotional disorders in women. Such as:

- hyper-vigilance,
- generalised anxiety,
- panic attacks,
- clinical depression
- and/or obsessive compulsive disorder.

Not to mention the possibility of making you more vulnerable to developing dementia as you grow older.

That's as a result of all that adrenaline washing around in your brain.

Apparently, it can damage the parts of the brain that help you access memories.

So. You owe it to yourself to work this thing through.

It doesn't have to hurt you any more.

With a pen and a notebook you can discover your story and work it all out.

You can spend less energy coping with unconscious, unexpressed feelings of fear and anxiety – and have energy for the people who deserve your love.

Your children, your family, your real friends.

BUT I DON'T WANT TO LEAVE HIM...

Well, that's your choice.

Maybe you love him too much to bail out.

Or you think your children would suffer if you broke up. It's up to you.

Write about it. Uncover it, discover it.

Many women stay with their emotionally abusive partner because they wouldn't classify him as an abuser.

Their accept his version of themselves as less them. They get caught up in self-blame.

They forget how to feel joy.

It isn't for me to tell you that you should leave a man who constantly undermines you.

This is a personal decision and always will be.

Even so, if you are a woman with an overwhelming sense of discomfort about certain patterns of controlling behaviour within your relationship; you can do the exercises in this book.

You can see if it's possible to find a way for your life to work anyway.

QUICK WRITE:

Write a letter to yourself.

Imagine your older self - she's looking at you right now, back down the years.

She's giving you good, loving advice about what to do next.

She wants the next story of your life to be beautiful. Full of love and good experiences.

Don't spend time thinking about this – just write.

Write fast and don't spend more than 10 minutes on it. Set a timer so you don't over-write.

Read this letter.

Discover what story your older self wants you to live.

Imagine how she wants you to get there.

Observe how she feels about you.

Then write a letter from your younger self.

Set a timer for 10 minutes.

How does she want her life to be?

What does she love?

What does she want to do?

Discover the stories of your older and younger selves.

Observe the way they feel.

Note down what you have found in this freewrite.

Remember this:

You can recover your sense of self-worth.

You can overcome the damage that's been done to the deepest and most essential parts of you.

But in order to do that it helps to understand exactly what is going on.

Armed with this knowledge, you can find a way to stop it from draining all your emotional resources.

QUICK WRITE:

List all the love songs you know.

You'll probably find that some of them are happy and some of them are sad.

Some of them suggest that love should hurt.

Do you agree?

How much hurt is too much in a loving relationship?

BETTER, PRETTIER, SEXIER...

After a while, emotionally abused women become obsessed by the relationship.

It consumes them.

They are caught in a cycle of constantly trying to fix themselves so they don't upset their partner.

They think if only they can be better, prettier, sexier, more hard working he'll love them all the time.

No. Nope. Nada. It won't happen. Sorry.

The more he points out your faults and the ways you let him down, the harder you'll try to please him.

And the more you fail.

This is how he controls you.

The cycle of abuse makes you lose sight of your own personal life. Why? Because most of your thinking time is spent working on the relationship.

Remember: Love doesn't have to hurt so much.

But what if you still believe that...

CHAPTER 7
MAYBE IT'S JUST A BAD PATCH?

"To heal the wound, you have to go into the dark night of the soul."
Tori Amos

IS IT JUST A BAD PATCH? IS THAT WHAT YOU THINK?

Well maybe you do.

Because how do you know the difference between a 'bad patch' and an abusive relationship?

FOR YEARS I TOLD MYSELF THIS STORY. *ONCE IT'S ALL FIXED, ONCE I do the right thing to please him, we'll be happy together.*

There are a lot of tell-tale signs to help you work out whether it's an abusive relationship or simply a difficult part of an otherwise healthy one.

Look at the list below and check off the ones that apply to you.

Five or more and this is much worse than a bad patch:

- If your working life is suffering because of the relationship difficulties
- If you're having trouble concentrating on simple tasks
- If you're losing interest in everything that used to give you pleasure
- If your life seems out of control and your partner is only interested in how it affects him
- If you feel like you spend most of your time desperately trying to please him in a way that fills you with despair and self-loathing
- If he calls you names, insults you, and uses abusive language whenever he wants to make a point – and you've grown used to this kind of abuse
- If your sex life is confusing, empty, and uncomfortable

ONE NOTE ON THAT LAST ONE.

Men can use sex as a weapon too.

He might refuse to have the kind of sex you like.

Or perhaps he pressures you to have sex too often or when you don't feel like it.

More seriously, does he expect you to engage in sexual activity that feels abusive, difficult or painful?

LONELINESS IS ALSO A PROBLEM FOR ABUSED WOMEN, FOR EXAMPLE:

- Do you feel more alone that you ever did when you were single?
- Do you feel like you're going mad when there's an argument?
- Do you feel confused and distracted a lot of the time?

CHAPTER 8
TURN YOUR WOUNDS INTO WISDOM

"She has fought many wars, most internal. The ones that you battle alone, for this, she is remarkable. She is a survivor." *Nikki Rowe*

QUICK WRITE:

Grab your notebook and pen a quiet five minutes. Imagine a wise old woman is sitting opposite you.

She's your inner wise woman or IWW.

Ask her this question:

I want to know who I am...

She knows the answer.

Let her freewrite it for you.

Use the first person.

Even if she says stuff like 'I'm the sand and the air and the hairs on a dog...' let her tell you what she knows. Don't think.

Follow the words.

Don't lift the pen off the paper.

Keep writing for 5 minutes.

Have a break.

Then write for another 5 minutes answering the same question.

Go deeper.

Dig.

IF YOU'VE HAD A WOLF IN YOUR BED - THE WOUNDS ARE ON THE inside.

And the wounds are deep.

An abusive wolf gives toxic love because he is incapable of real love.

In his mind, *he is relating to you as his inferior*.

HE EXPECTS A HANDMAID OF UNLIMITED PERFECTION.

There is no such thing.

What does this do to you? Well, after a few years of toxic love you've probably forgotten who you are.

A QUICK WORD ABOUT YOUR INNER WISE WOMAN OR IWW.

She's imaginary but she's real at the same time.

She's a part of you – the really balanced, spiritual and loving part.

She's like a mixture of your fairy godmother, guardian angel and the village herbalist.

She's a healer and she looks out for you.

She's your intuition, your rational self combined with your feeling self.

She's always on your side.

BUT YOU'VE GROWN DISTANT FROM HER.

Emotional abuse does that in a number of ways.

Mostly it's just because you've been thinking about your wolf all the time.

It feels like you're trying to fix the relationship - but actually you're working through a cloud of confusion. His abuse causes that.

It's called crazy-making.

Confusion cuts you off from your own feelings and consequently, your intuition, your emotional compass.

Cut off from your own feelings – you stop listening to your IWW.

This makes you more vulnerable, more alone. And easier to break down.

Wolves will always use confusion – it's their main weapon.

So, your IWW needs to get back in touch.

You don't need any special meditations, incense, candles, music or whatever to get in contact with her.

All you need is:

- A pen and a notebook.
- The knowledge that she's right there
- A question to ask her
- A few minutes to freewrite her answer.

CHAPTER 9
SIGNS OF ABUSE CHECKLISTS

"One way to locate your most urgent subjects is to ask yourself, 'Where is my heart breaking?' or 'What breaks my heart?'..."
Rebecca McClanahan

OKAY, WE'VE HAD A QUICK RUN-THOUGH OF SOME SHORT checklists. Now here's the real thing.

I've brought together everything I could find on emotionally abusive behaviour and put it all together.

Read through the checklists that follow and circle each statement that is true for you.

Abusive behaviour is consistent over a long period of time. Just as an example of how well these lists work - I asked a friend of mine to complete them.

She's been in a very long and happy marriage.

She answered 'no' to all but two of the statements.

Based on my last relationship which was with an emotionally abusive wolf, I answered 'yes' to all but two.

If you get a high number of 'yes' answers – don't worry. Remember:

an emotionally abusive man will be generous and loving at the start of a relationship.

You're not a fool for falling in love. It's a great gift to be able to love so wholeheartedly and fully.

If you score five or more true points on each list you are probably living with an abusive man.

VERBAL ABUSE CHECKLIST:
He often:

- Calls me disgusting names.
- Withholds important information from me so that I don't understand what's going on.
- Confuses me by lying about things we've said or done together.
- Messes up my head so I can't trust my own thoughts.
- Puts me down when we're alone.
- Puts me down in public or in front of my children.
- Trivialises things which are important to me or the things I'm interested in.
- Harasses me about stupid things when I'm tired.
- Interrogates me to the point where I'm exhausted.
- Accuses me of things I haven't done.
- Twists my words so that I'm to blame when he's upset me.
- Blames me for the problems in our relationship.
- Accuses me of not loving him properly.
- Blocks my point of view by talking over me.
- Refuses to let me discuss my feelings with him.
- Diverts attention away from the awful things he's said to me.
- Tells me lies.
- Taunts me when I'm upset.
- Discounts my feelings or opinions.
- Threatens to harm me/the children/our pets in some way.
- Makes hurtful jokes which put me down.

- Yells at me without provocation.
- Rages so much that I'm frightened of him.
- Uses sarcastic comments to let me know what he thinks about me.

EMOTIONAL ABUSE CHECKLIST:
He often:

- Doesn't care, or is even angry with me when I'm feeling low.
- Doesn't care or is angry with me when I'm ill.
- Withholds affection from me when I need it most.
- Withholds sex from me when he knows I'm interested.
- Wants sex when I'm not interested.
- Says he wants the kind of sex that he knows turns me off.
- Acts like he's the victim in our relationship.
- Seems to be competing with me when we should be working together.
- Gives me dirty looks for no reason.
- Ignores me or gives me the silent treatment
- Is very attentive to other people but not to me.
- Showers attention on other women in front of me.
- Goes on about things he finds attractive or interesting in others.
- Talks kindly about other women and not about me.
- Seems to feel better after he's had a go at me.
- Wants sex after he's really hurt my feelings.
- Is really, really nice for a while – but it never lasts.
- Doesn't listen to me when I'm talking.
- Makes it clear that he wouldn't behave like this if I wasn't such a difficult person to live with.

THERE. YOU'VE DONE IT. I KNOW HOW HARD IT IS TO LOOK through these lists.

I found it difficult to read them, put them together and even to write them down.

Why?

Well, it's difficult because you don't want it to be true. You may find yourself feeling foolish because you let this happen. Don't. You didn't know the rules of the game. Now you do.

It's especially hard if you still love him.

However, remember the stuff about traumatic bonding?

It doesn't mean you're not in love. It just means he's messed with your love and it's become – damaged. Like milk left out in the sun.

If you've been with a wolf you'll find his behaviour much more shocking when you see it written down.

But think about it.

That just shows the power of words.

And you're going to learn how to harness this power.

With this power you can change everything. Make your new life, mend the broken bits. Start loving and caring for yourself first – and then be able to give that love to those who deserve it.

Your children. Your family. Your friends. Your self.

CHAPTER 10
ON FAIRY RINGS

"...the fairies dance in a place apart,
    Shaking their milk-white feet in a ring..."
    W. B. Yeats

WHY FAIRY RINGS ARE BAD FOR YOUR HEALTH

Of course fairy rings don't actually exist.

My granny used to call those rings of mushrooms sprouting out of her lawn - 'fairy rings'.

Originally people believed they were gateways into another world. The Otherworld. A Fairyland of sorts – but not the kind you would tell a child about.

Oh no. Not the Disney version.

The Otherworld was a dangerous place where the best you could expect was to become a slave. It was easy to make a mistake in this land and if you upset a senior fairy or elven king – the consequences might be deadly.

Often, so the legends go, the humans who went there could never return.

It was all wonderful at first.

Lots of dancing, singing, sex and general partying. But everything turned sour sooner or later. Parties have a way of wearing you out if they go on too long. You can end up hung-over, drained, and in desperate need of somewhere peaceful to lie down - preferably in the dark.

But inside the fairy ring you're a prisoner and you're there to follow the rules.

Sounds familiar?

Well it is if you've been in a relationship with a wolf. There's a sense that the relationship has plunged you into a dark place. And it isn't comfortable or happy or nice.

You'll know exactly what I'm talking about.

When you fell in love with him you stepped into the fairy ring and entered into another world.

It's a world of confusion and magic in equal doses.

In the end, all the confusion makes you feel crazy. And you have to do what you're told. You're enchanted. You're enslaved. You're in a prison with invisible walls.

WELCOME TO THE WORLD OF THE WOLF.

Here, all *ladies* must be fragrant princesses – almost comatose in their submissive desire to please him.

They don't get sick or have opinions or – heaven forfend – disagree with his unwritten, sacred and confusing rules.

BREAKING OUT IS HARD TO DO

The pagan ancestors of northern Europe saw fairy rings as a very bad thing.

In those days everyone knew they must never enter a fairy ring.

They were often found on the top of burial mounds – those lumpy hills dotted around the British Isles and beyond.

These were the places where the dead danced along with the fae.

So, if you heard music playing at night in the vicinity of a fairy ring the best thing you could do was run home as fast as you could. The music would be so captivating it would be hard to resist.

Like a lover whispering in your ear.

But if you drifted into the dance, you'd be transported to another world. And you might never escape.

Or you'd dance for what seemed like a few hours but when it was over, you'd find years had passed, your hair was grey and all your loved ones were dead.

EITHER WAY, IT WAS AN ENCHANTMENT BEST AVOIDED, HOWEVER fun it might be for a while.

Eventually you would be enslaved in the Otherworld, or prematurely aged in this one.

Escaping from this place was always thought to be really difficult, if not impossible. Remember Stockholm Syndrome? Their emotional captivity lasted well beyond their actual ordeal.

Sometimes, when people did escape from a fairy ring – they pined away because they couldn't stop thinking about it. They were addicted, even though it hurt them to be there.

So the Otherworld had a hold over them – it was like a gilded cage. Alcatraz with good interior design, twinkly lights and plenty of drum and bass.

Somehow, you know you have to get away. But you're enchanted. Hypnotised by its dreamy qualities.

It's great to feel like a princess even if it's only some of the time.

Even if the rest of the time you're an emotional punch-bag.

This is why it's such a struggle to leave the world your wolf has made for you.

It's an illusion.

And it suits him more than it suits his chosen prey.

You know it's not right and it hurts to be there.

And it hurts to leave.

Also, many wolves have complete financial control over a woman's life. The fear of having to deal with all that stuff is a powerful enchantment.

By the way – you don't have to leave him to leave his world.

Of course, it's much harder to stay with him and not buy into his vision. But it can be done. You just have to work much harder. You have to remind him that when he insults you or puts you down in public or shouts vile abuse at you that it's not okay.

Every single time.

HOW YOU BECOME TRAPPED IN HIS WORLD...

Easy. He promised you a rose garden. Or – more likely – a life of loving companionship, excitement and fulfilling sex.

At first, he acted like he was your soul mate. You didn't need anyone else.

Remember the early days? Great, weren't they?

At first he's an angel. The closest friend you ever had. He laughed at all your jokes. He was an attentive lover.

Like the music from an enchanted world, his love at the beginning will overwhelm you.

Wolves don't play the love game by halves. They know which song to play, how to make you feel special. How to get in your bed.

He won't show his true colours by insulting you with foul language on the first date.

Those of us who have loved abusive men do not fall in love with his dark side.

We are introduced to it gradually.

We are dazzled by the light first.

Maybe for a long time now you've been struggling with guilt. Guilt about falling in love with the kind of man who treats you like dirt.

Well don't.

Why? Because...

HE'S A CON-ARTIST...

You only need to feel bad about the things that were in your control.

He lessened your ability to control your life because he took control of as much of your life as he could.

He trapped you inside his story.

Symbolically he stole you away from your real life as a whole person.

Then, oh so slowly, he took you deep down to a place of fear - a place where even the strongest human heart would tremble.

WHEN THE RELATIONSHIP IS ESTABLISHED AND HE IS SECURE IN YOUR love for him, the abuse begins.

You've entered the ring of his enchantment and it's very hard to stop dancing.

By the time the relationship is a going thing - you'll have told everyone how wonderful he is.

It's hard to admit you were wrong.

Even to yourself.

Besides, he will still be lovely.

Sometimes.

On top of that, you'll be oddly isolated from the people who really love you.

A wolf finds a way to drive a wedge between you and your closest friends and family.

Slowly, his moods became the centre of your life. Sometimes he is once again the fantastic guy you fell for. But more and more often, he lets you know he despises you.

He makes it clear that everything you think and say and do is wrong. Every part of you, physical, emotional or spiritual is ridiculed or belittled in some way.

By this time you are in too deep to get out easily.

There's only room in the relationship for his world-view.

You try harder and harder to please him. The guilt grows. But the more you do to try to change yourself to please him, the more drained and exhausted you become.

Perhaps you give in to sex when you don't want it; or take part in sexual acts that make you feel uncomfortable.

You push your boundaries so far that in the end - you don't know who you are any more.

He confuses you to the point where it feels like you're crazy.

One woman was bullied into never discussing the fact that her husband almost killed her.

It was during a scuba diving expedition. He made sure that *she* felt too guilty and ashamed of what *he* had done to ever bring the subject up. It would have upset *him* too much.

This kind of manipulation and mind control feels like a kind of dark magic.

Like the spell cast over Sleeping Beauty when she pricks her finger on the spindle. During this phase of the relationship, you fall asleep to your own needs.

QUICK WRITE:

> Write the words:
> '**The first time we met...**' at the top of a new page.
> Give it 5 minutes.
> It's good to remember how great it was.
> You're not stupid to fall in love with a man like that.
> It's also good to remember that a wolf never feels love.
> He's just an expert at faking it.

JUST TO RECAP:

- In the beginning the wolf will have charmed, delighted and enraptured you with his overwhelming love.
- Sadly, once he feels secure enough in the relationship to morph into his true self; the charm will turn sour;
- But by then it's too late.
- Some wolves are harder to leave than others, possibly because they might turn violent
- If you believe he could turn violent, get help. Phone the

police, a women's helpline, a priest or someone else
you trust.

IN THE DAYS WHEN WOLVES LIVED IN FORESTS AND WERE A REAL
threat to human life, we learned to be afraid of them.

And in many cultures they became a symbol of voracious appetite,
demonic presence and dangerous sexual appetites.

Real wolves are wild animals of great beauty and grace. Using the
symbolic, demonic wolf of fairy tales you can understand the deep
psychology of certain types of emotional abuse.

And through writing you can:

Discover your story.

Imagine a new ending.

Observe your feelings and actions more accurately.

Love your life again.

That's the way to turn wounds into wisdom.

What happens once you've been trapped in his world?

"I AM VERY SORRY SAD FOR MEN AND WOMEN TRAPPED IN ANY
relationship where there is cruelty, dominance, inequity. I long for the
liberation of all people." *Jasmine Guy*

In his world you're not you. No, you've got a role to play – a role
you never get to choose.

This role is based on his bizarre vision of what women are like. You
and I know that not all women are alike. We have different personalities. We go through life changes and have our off days. We fart in bed
or fall asleep while he's talking. It doesn't mean we don't love him. It
just means we're human.

Not in fairyland. You're supposed to be a princess, dammit.

In the original version of Sleeping Beauty – the prince rapes her while she's asleep. More than that, he actually thinks she's dead. If you read the chapter on Sleeping Beauty and discover that this is your dominant fairy story – then your man is only attracted to you when you are very quiet and hardly moving.

No wonder you could never please him.

Don't forget – **these patterns are not your faulty relationship patterns.**

They are his.

ONCE YOU ARE LIVING FULLY IN THE WORLD YOUR WOLF HAS created for you

- he loses interest. Why? Because he's bored. After all, he has the power he craves. He's won. He still owns you and he might be possessively jealous. But he lets his guard down more often and abuses you whenever he needs to let off steam.

You're not as interesting because you are no longer allowed to be yourself. This is because he doesn't see you as an individual person with thoughts and feelings of your own. Instead, you're playing a role which fits his two-dimensional view of womankind. In the words of a song – you're a puppet on a string.

And you'll always be a disappointment because let's be realistic here – no living person is content being a puppet on the end of a load of strings. You're not so much fun dangling there looking a bit worn out and confused.

In fairy tales the female characters often appear to suffer without complaint. It's as though they accept their fate willingly. They don't seem to have much of a personality. Actually, in some of the older versions of the stories they fight back and are cunning and brave. But most of these tales have been changed to reflect a certain moral and cultural viewpoint of women.

This view of the perfect female portrays her as passive, pure, child-like and bland. Once you've entered his Otherworld you are supposed to act like this. You may well feel you are disappearing as an individual. This is because to an abusive man, the real you might as well disappear.

He's only let you into his world so he can play with you for a while. Once he's got control and power he needs to make it more challenging. But once you're worn out – you're no fun to play with. He might not want to let you go. But that's because he owns you. Not because he loves you.

If he's got money you'll be trapped in a golden tower. If he's poor, you'll be trapped by his demands.

Either way, it's as if you are slowly being drained of your life force.

This is how humans suffered if they entered the fairy ring.

A fairy tale might seem simple. But often they hide complex psychological truths – ones which are as useful today as they always were. So this is why fairy tales matter.

CHAPTER 11
FAIRY TALES MATTER...

"...fairy tales provide a unique window into our most central concerns, our sense of social and cultural identity, who we think we are (or should be) – and how we change...

Catherine Orenstein

WHAT CATHERINE ORNSTEIN IS SAYING IS THIS:

- Fairy tales are a mirror reflecting the deepest part of ourselves
- If we study them, play around with them – we can see what really matters to us such as:
- Where we fit in, socially
- What our attitudes, beliefs and desires are
- Who we really are
- And who we might become.

Fairy stories were around a very long time before they were written down. They shift and change because for so long they were passed down by word of mouth. They pop up in all cultures. And often they have the same themes.

Some people think they may have always been with us.

When you fall, you need to land on familiar ground.

Fairy tales, if nothing else, are as familiar as it gets.

WHICH STORY PATTERN FITS YOUR EXPERIENCE BEST?

Is it lack of imagination?

I don't know, but most emotionally abusive wolves have a limited repertoire.

QUICK WRITE:

10 minutes.

Grab your notebook, computer or a scrap of paper and make a list of all the fairy tales you know.

Look back over them.

Were they read aloud to you as a child?

Did you see a Disney movie of the tale and love it as a child?

Have you read them to your own children?

Which one was your favourite?

Write down the feelings you had about this story as a child.

IN HIS MIND HE'LL BE CASTING YOU IN A ROLE.

You'll be Little Red Riding Hood one day and Karen from The Red Shoes the next.

So all the stories will seem to fit.

However, your wolf will have one main script he keeps returning to.

You might already have some idea of what that script or fairy tale or pattern might be.

Who have you become since your wolf got in your bed?

- A girl on the wrong path through the woods?

- A woman whose tongue has been cut out?
- A passive princess who sleeps as the prince rapes her?

AND WHO DO YOU THINK YOU SHOULD BE?

This is the most important question to ask yourself.

And you can answer it most effectively through writing.

Perhaps you feel you'd like to be:

- A wily maiden taking revenge on her captor?
- A she-wolf outrunning the wolf in granny's clothing?
- A mermaid who goes back to the sea alive – and takes the prince's golden crown with her?
- A princess who boots out the arrogant prince and runs the castle just the way she likes it?
- A maid in red shoes who dances to her own tune?

LONG AGO IN A LAND FAR AWAY

Stories are as flexible as wool.

We can spin a yarn any old way we choose; we can even spin gold from flax. Why not?

Even your own story is yours to re-write. Even if it feels as though you've lost control and your life is a mess.

In one sense it's as though the oldest stories we have are the ones that tell us the most about ourselves. Perhaps fairy stories are the keys that open the door to the unconscious mind. At least as much as dreams do anyway.

But why would we want to open those doors?

Perhaps - to find knowledge, insight and to discover how to change.

Those are really important reasons to go there, down into the dark and creepy basement of our own minds.

IT'S ALL ABOUT THE SYMBOLS.

Fairy tales are as full of these as dreams. They've been around so long we recognise the images; the wolves waiting in the woods, poor little Cinders and her fairy Godmother.

In ancient times it was practical to warn children to stay out of the forest where hungry wolves prowled.

Fairy tales often give animals human qualities.

The wolf is a symbol of the manipulative charmer, the seducer, the man who sees women as prey. The narcissist, the sociopath – somehow we all know what a wolf-man is - even if we can't spot him right away.

Young girls learned these truths from elder women in the tribe and took them into womanhood.

By looking at these stories again, we can see so much more. We can take what we need from them and find what is most useful for us.

In fact, it's probably true to say that originally these stories were never meant to be for children. But because we've grown up with the watered down versions they have a playful, distant feel to them.

'*Long ago in a land far away...*'

WHAT DO WE FIND THERE?

- talking animals,
- shape shifters,
- princesses,
- castles,
- fairies,
- ogres,
- magic,
- witches
- magicians
- evil dragons
- greedy princes
- evil step-mothers
- despotic kings and so on.

NONE OF IT IS REAL. IT'S FANTASY.

And that's why fairy tales with can help you see our own story in a more detached way.

Think of your fairy story as a protective blanket.

Hide under it as long as you need to.

The fairy tales chosen for this book are often violent and surreal.

They're like horror movies taking place in a dream landscape.

Everything there is surreal and upside-down.

We find transvestite wolves, severed feet that dance, cannibalism, a mermaid whose tongue has been torn out and a man with blue facial hair who likes to murder his wives.

These are often the original tales - or the versions of tales you would definitely not tell a small child.

However, this dreamlike quality makes them brilliant tools when it comes to dealing with emotions.

SCIENCE HAS COME A LONG WAY IN RESEARCHING THE BRAIN AND discovering how we think.

But when it comes to our emotions there is still more mystery than real understanding.

Your most complex feelings cannot be shown in an equation.

What makes one person cry makes another one laugh.

Symbols, characters and events: these are the things that help us unravel our emotional lives.

Stories are safe holding bays.

They hold up a mirror to the storms inside reflecting the truth in a way we can handle.

As you read each tale and learn more about the wolf in your bed, remember: you're on the outside looking in.

The wolf devours the grandmother – the future soul of Red Riding Hood.

You, on the other hand, can reclaim your soul. Imagine a new ending.

Slice Little Red out of the belly of the wolf.

Make sure no one ever marries Bluebeard by showing his true self to the world.

Break free.

Love your life.

THE POWER OF STORIES

"...all storytelling, consciously or not, follows the ancient patterns of myth..."

The Writer's Journey; Christopher Vogler

STORIES, JOURNEYS AND FINDING TREASURE

Stories are there for a reason. Sure, they entertain us. But it's much more than that.

They have a purpose.

They inspire, warn and teach us things about ourselves.

They are probably as important to our psychological well-being as good food and exercise is to our physical health.

This is because, through stories:

- we try out other lives,
- new perspectives,
- alternative ways of living,
- of loving
- of leaving –
- all from the safety of a chair, bus or beach towel.

From literary novels to bestsellers - every type of story has one thing in common.

The main character, our hero, is a person in a setting with a problem. She goes on a journey. She may go on a trip round the world, into the dark woods or travel no further than the nearest supermarket.

Her journey might be into her own heart or the jungles of Brazil.

What prompts this journey is always a sense that something is missing.

Red Riding Hood is missing a grandmother.

Bridget Jones is missing a life partner.

Indiana Jones is always missing an artefact of great historical significance.

FINDING THE TREASURE

At some point in every story the main character finds treasure.

In the external world they might find a lost child. Or money or love or redemption or a way out of prison. The treasure is often also a wound which needs to heal in the internal world of your main character.

They might find that the thing they wanted so much − doesn't matter to them anymore. Not after the journey and all they've discovered along the way. In that case, the treasure they've found is something invisible − something internal. Transformation.

Their transformation takes place through an epiphany, an experience of great insight.

When the ending is happy we are left with new knowledge or understanding about how to tackle certain obstacles well.

In a tragedy, the main character dies or is rejected and the treasure is withheld from them. We are left trying to work out how we would have succeeded where they failed.

Like the Little Mermaid, pining away for love.

It seemed as though she had her treasure at the beginning. By that I mean her underwater Kingdom. But frolicking with her loving family was not enough for her. She falls in love and the prince becomes her new treasure. But it all goes horribly wrong in the original version.

Her story is a tragedy.

She loses everything. The prince rejects her and her treasure is gone, out of reach. We are moved − emotionally - when she dies and turns into foam.

And music is similar.

Music is like storytelling. Every song rises out of a different arrangement of the same few notes. Music makes us feel something. Stories – if they're any good – make us feel something too.

They also have relatively few notes.

Characters, setting, a problem, a wound to heal, and a goal to strive for.

A Knight finds the Holy Grail and we feel bliss for a brief moment.

A poor serving maid marries a prince and we feel all warm and fuzzy inside.

A girl dressed in red is eaten by a wolf. We feel outraged.

WHY DO WE GET SO MUCH PLEASURE FROM STORIES? WELL, FOR ONE thing, they give events and characters a proper shape.

A place to go. A treasure to pursue. They tidy up the random chaos of our lives. Crime novels give us poetic justice. Good defeats evil.

Fairy tales go a lot deeper although they've been there in our lives for so long. They taught us as children in some strange way, how to feel things.

All our emotions are felt and interpreted in the brain. Strangely enough, heartbreak can produce a real physical pain in the middle of the chest, somewhere around the heart. This is why when we talk about love we often talk about the heart.

We're not really talking about the muscular pump the size of a fist essential to circulation. It's a symbol. But we all know by now that it's with our mind we fall in love, experience pain, joy and all the blended colours of emotions.

Perhaps it's more accurate to say that the heart is a part of the mind.

A part that holds the key to making our life meaningful.

So, we can use our mind to access the real power of the heart. The power to recover. To imagine a place beyond the suffering.

Your mind, your imagination - can set you free.

And it's with this, your heart-mind, that you start to love your life again.

QUICK WRITE:

Pick your favourite movie about love and watch it right through.

Write down the answers to these three questions in your notebook:

What kind of journey does the main character go on?

What is missing from her/his life at the start?

What treasure does she/he gain in the end?

Also note down what kind of emotions you feel when you watch this movie.

This is an exercise you can return to many times while you work with this book.

Your favourite film will change according to your mood and how you feel about life, love the universe and everything.

Notice how you're changing through your choice of story, character and journey.

CHAPTER 12
SCRIPT THEORY

"Story, as it turns out, was crucial to our evolution—more so than opposable thumbs. Opposable thumbs let us hang on; story told us what to hang on to."

Lisa Cron

SCIENTISTS ARE BEGINNING TO THINK THAT STORIES ARE NOT JUST pleasant indulgences.

The psychologist, Roger Schank, came up with the idea of script theory. It's a brilliant idea.

Basically, he suggested that stories are the shape they are because they help us remember things. Every story has a sort of script – a beginning, a middle and an end.

He thought that story scripts exist from birth in our brains. They're like empty scripts with spaces for us to fill in. Like some kind of built- in 'story skeleton', story slots or *story understanding mechanism*.

You use them to make sense of everything.

In other words, a new born baby has a basic idea of the shape of life experiences.

There's a beginning, a middle and an end. A character, a setting and a problem. A few years go by and she builds these up into useful stuff.

You go into a restaurant, you order food, you eat food, you pay and you leave.

The End.

Boy meets girl. Something keeps them apart. Girl and boy sort out their problems, and live more or less happily ever after.

The End.

Of course, the details change according to who you eat with and what the food and service are like – but the restaurant script or story skeleton fits most restaurant situations. The structure is there and you fill in the blanks.

More recently, Turner describes story as '... *the central principal of our experience and knowledge...*'. He talks about story frameworks as part of the basic structure of all human knowledge.

He even thought they might be physically detectable in the neural wiring of the brain.

Wow! Story structure in the brain. I'd love to see an image of that some day. The inner story, nestling in among all that biology.

But the main point is this: your brain is hard-wired to think, feel and make sense of the world through stories.

So, in this book I've decided to make good use of the natural way we think i.e. in story form – to help people recover from the trauma of emotional abuse.

I've used fairy tales as a way of talking about the patterns of behaviour that occur in abusive relationships.

Many original fairy stories were far more gruesome and dark than the ones we tell our children nowadays. And most of the tales I've used here are set out in their grimmest form.

There are many truths locked inside fairy tales.

Truths we can use for understanding and healing.

CHAPTER 13
THE HEALING GIFT OF WRITING

"...look in thy heart
And write - ..."
Carol Ann Duffy

WRITING AS THERAPY

Writers have known for years that writing is good for you. Trouble is - they don't always use it well.

Proper writers, by that I mean serious novelists and poets and suchlike, often dance at the edge of their own sanity.

So maybe they're not such a good example.

Paradoxically, many of them agree that writing keeps them sane. It keeps them healthy in some mysterious way.

Perhaps all writers would be totally bonkers if they didn't write.

By writing they manage to remain just a bit weird some of the time instead of totally weird the entire time.

However. There's been a lot of work recently looking at the health benefits of writing.

All you have to do is write down how you truly feel and what you really think. There's no need to be an 'author' working on the next prizewinning literary masterpiece.

You just write what matters to you, from the heart.

WE OFTEN THINK THAT IN ORDER FOR SOMETHING TO WORK IT HAS to be hard. Most things in reality *are* like that.

To become an author takes years of studying the art and craft of writing, sitting alone in a room trying not to go mad. Add to that a modicum of talent and a big dose of luck – and you might just churn out a book that sells.

But if you only want to sort out your feelings and recover from heartbreak, all you have to do is buy a notebook and scribble away for a few minutes at a time.

You don't have to do it every day although it helps to start off like.

After a while you can just write down your feelings when you have a lot of them.

A bit like letting off steam in a controlled environment.

No need ignore your feelings. No need to squash them down so they fester away. That can make you sick in the end. No need to act out every emotion flitting through you. That can make the people around you sick in the end.

WRITING STRENGTHENS YOUR BODY...

Surprising – but true.

In 1997 James W. Pennebaker wrote a paper about the therapeutic benefits of writing about emotions.

He designed a nice simple experiment to test his idea that writing about emotional trauma had a positive healing effect.

He found that by writing freely about their darkest moments - the participants in his study improved their immune systems.

Amazing! This alone is striking, especially since the measures looked at things like antibody levels and natural killer cell activity – showing that the effect was biological – but what about the psychological effects?

AND YOUR MIND...

Those who took part in the study also showed a marked increase in their grades if they were students.

They were more likely to find work if they were unemployed. They drank less alcohol if they were heavy drinkers.

And they recorded less absenteeism from work.

Basically they were stronger in mind and body.

They were coping better with stress.

They were opening up to the world as it is.

In his report on the study Pennebaker wrote that:

"...in general, writing about emotional topics is associated with significant reductions in stress..."

A NOTEBOOK, A PEN AND A QUIET FIVE MINUTES...

"I don't want to live in a hand-me-down world of others' experiences. I want to write about me, my discoveries, my fears, my feelings, about me."

Helen Keller

DOTTED AROUND IN THE FIRST FEW CHAPTERS OF THIS BOOK ARE some 'Quick Write' ideas.

You may or may not have done any of them.

If you did, you've already started the process of therapeutic writing.

If you haven't tried any yet, here's an easy one.

QUICK WRITE

Set a timer for 10 minutes.

Write this sentence at the top of a new page:

The hardest I ever had to deal with was...

Write as fast as you can.

Don't think about what you write.

If you get stuck, just repeat the same sentence such as 'I don't know what to write' until something new appears.

Trust what emerges.

THAT'S ALL THERE IS TO IT. THAT'S FREEWRITING.

It's like freewheeling a bicycle down a hill or shooting the breeze with a close friend over a bottle of wine.

- It's simple and profound.
- It's poetry and nonsense.
- It's like being lost and found at the same time.
- Read it over – and discover the diamonds in the dust.

DIAMONDS IN THE DUST

This is the key to kicking the wolf out of your bed and more importantly – out of your head.

The more you practise discernment in the privacy of your own notebook, and spot the diamonds in your own thoughts, the more you chuck out the dust - then the easier it'll be to spot a wolf in the future.

You get to make informed choices.

You're in control of your life – on the page of your notebook at first and then – for real.

On the page you can feel anything and say anything and think anything and it's okay.

Your unconscious mind won't let you write anything you can't handle.

You might write about something that moves you to tears but that's because you're ready to cry.

You might write about something that suddenly seems funny instead of sad and that's because you're ready to laugh.

When you first start writing it's best to freewrite.

Later on, we'll start spinning yarns and putting stories together.

Gradually you'll write snippets of stories.

Eventually, you might even want to write your wolf story in full. You might want to turn it into a novel and get published. If so, go for it. It's up to you.

Write what you need.

You'll surprise, shock and delight yourself with your creativity.

You'll be absorbed like a child and yet some of the stuff you write will be wise beyond your years.

This is because there is a child inside you.

There's also a wise woman and a kindly old man and a high priestess and a joker and a warrior.

QUICK WRITE:

If you haven't already, go shopping for a notebook.

Find one you like, I mean *really* like. This is for you. It's about reclaiming your inner self.

Take your time.

Enjoy choosing this wonderful object. It doesn't have to be expensive or have a serious cover. Better if it doesn't. It just has to feel right.

Make sure it fits in your bag or purse. Also, make sure you get a pen that you like. Imagine how good it will feel to finally say what you want to say.

Treat yourself to a nice cup of coffee or tea.

Open the page (the next page if you've already treated yourself to a notebook) and write the date and the words:

If I was lost in the woods I'd find my way out by...

Then write anything that comes into your head for 5 minutes.

Don't take your pen off the page.

Don't check your grammar or spelling or try to write 'properly'.

Just write the words as they come.

Even if you repeat the same words over and over. You'll get through that.

Write about how it feels to be lost.

Write about the thoughts you might have as darkness falls.

Write about loneliness or skinning a rabbit to survive. Write about losing your phone, making a fire - the sounds of wild animals.

Write about fear.

Write about loneliness.

Write about rain or the sound of a waterfall.

Keep writing. It's only 5 minutes. When you've finished − drink coffee.

QUICK WRITE

5 Minutes:

Write the titles of your favourite films/books/plays/songs at the top of the page.

It can be anything, historical, romance, cult flick, literary masterpiece etc.

Pick the best scene − the one that made the biggest impression on you.

Explore what it means to you for 5 minutes.

These stories, songs, movies, plays are all facets of who you are.

If you can't remember the best scene or moment − watch the film or read the book/play again.

Freewrite what happens in this scene.

Was somebody rescued?

Did the main character speak her mind at last?

Did she find redemption?

Did she fall in love?

Let go?

Make everyone laugh?

Run away into the sunset on her trusty horse?

Read back what you wrote.

Did you name any feelings? If so − which ones?

Does anything in this scene have echoes with your own life?

Does the main character do something you've always wanted to do but didn't feel brave enough?

Can you imagine a different ending to this scene?

If you find yourself identifying with many characters, it doesn't mean you've got a split personality.

We're all a mixture of 'characters'.

The psychologist Jung said we all have access to inner archetypes. The Fool. The Queen. The Wise Woman. The Stern King. The High Priestess. The Fairy Godmother.

That's why they pop up in fairy tales and in all stories one way or another.

They're inside us first. Gather your allies. And begin to think of yourself as a hero...

YOU ARE THE MAIN CHARACTER IN YOUR LIFE

In the bustle and pressure of daily life it's easy to forget who you are.

If you are living with or have lived with an emotionally abusive wolf - you will have such a low opinion of yourself that forgetting who you are is the easiest way to cope.

QUICK WRITE

10 minutes.

Imagine for a moment that your life is a movie.

You only have one viewpoint.

Your own.

You can't see what goes on behind closed doors with any of the other characters in your life.

You have to rely on hearsay and anecdotes for that.

You're looking at yourself from a safe distance.

You are the hero [this word can mean a male or female character], the main character in the story of your life.

Write a quick synopsis of how your life is right now.

Afterwards, read back what you've written.

If you feel that you're not yet living the life you'd like for yourself, remember this:

One single life is not single story.

Your life is made up of many stories.

There's the story of your first family holiday, the story of your first love, the story of your career, the story of the wolf in your bed...

PUTTING THE TWO TOGETHER:

So, now you know a bit about how your brain filters everything that happens to you through story scripts.

You also know that writing about your feelings and thoughts is good for psychological health.

Freewriting is great and easy and free.

And the positive effects are clear but it seems to leave out something obvious.

Story.

Your story.

Not just the real story of your life with an abusive man, but also the fictional, creative bits. The daydreams, the hopes – the fears.

Your mind is not just rooted in the ordinary details of each day. It's underpinned by your imagination.

Your dreams at night and your daydreaming – those moments of private, story-shaped thinking.

I'm bound to be drawn to this side of the human mind. After all, I'm a creative writing teacher as well as a psychology graduate and it seems like the two things – creative storytelling and freewriting fit together like a key in the right lock.

Out of curiosity and because I too woke up one morning and realised there was a wolf in my bed, I wanted to extend the ideas of narrative psychology.

To do that, I researched what happened when the two things are put together.

Freewriting for health using an imaginative story-like structure.

I discovered they work very well.

Our ancestors probably knew this.

That's almost certainly how fairy tales started out.

It begins with the truth. A true story of a girl lost in the woods. She is stalked, seduced and killed by a strange man. Over time and with lots of re-telling, the girl dons a red cloak with a hood and the man becomes a wolf.

In some versions, Little Red Riding Hood fights him off. In others she dies. And sometimes she's rescued by a passing hunter.

The characters are there – the young woman, the stranger, the sense of menace. But what happens to them – the end of the story – is flexible.

A Very Sturdy Ladder

So far, much of the work on writing therapy has used the technique of freewriting.

You choose a topic, for example; the worst day of my life, and write freely without thinking for five, ten or twenty minutes.

Pennebaker's instructions to the participants in his experiment outline this approach:

"...I would like you to write about your very deepest thoughts and feelings about an extremely important emotional issue that has affected you and your life. In your writing, I'd like you to really let go and explore your very deepest emotions and thoughts..."

You could try this exercise too.

Write for 10 minutes.

The effect Pennebaker found were brilliant. **Just through doing this one simple exercise, people's lives improved**.

They were healthier, happier and more able to cope.

He told them not to worry about spelling, grammar or structure.

Freewriting from a deep place is an exercise that many creative writers use on an almost daily basis to limber up for a session of prose or poetry writing. It helps loosen you as a writer and tends to encourage the flow of words.

But when I came across Louise DeSalvo's book 'Writing as a Way of Healing' I could see how much better it is to go beyond the initial splurge of free writing.

She says that writing is:

"... a very sturdy ladder out of the Pit to reach freedom and safety..."

She then goes on to outline a process for writing the story of your experiences.

I pulled out my notes for this book, and realised that this was the same conclusion I'd come to, although my method is different.

It seems so intuitively correct that storytelling with a real structure could be more helpful than just getting a mass of words down on the page.

After all, if our minds understand our world primarily through stories, and writing has healing qualities, then using the two of them together must be pretty damn good.

How this Book Works:

This book works because you put the work in.

Now you've understood the healing power of stories and writing – you're going to tackle the two main ingredients of any story.

Character and plot.

You're the main character, the hero in your story – but you'll have to understand your wolf better to write your way home. He's the villain, the antagonist. The one who promotes growth and healing in the hero if she can outdo him.

When it comes to wolves there are two truths.

One is that they're all the same. They act the way they do based on shared, core beliefs about women.

And secondly, they're different. In fact, research has found that they fall into several distinct character types.

Don't worry if your wolf falls into more than one – the questionnaires later on will sort out his dominant type.

After that, we'll go on to look at the fairy nightmare your wolf type is most likely to have chosen for you to live in.

Then we'll work the rest of the **DIOL** method to write your way home.

Home to the place where you belong; the place where you love the life you live.

We'll do this by:

Discovering the story that fits your experience. This step is a moment of truth.

Imagining a new ending – one which satisfies you. This step gets you back in touch with your intuitive self.

Observing your feelings as they grow stronger. This step is an ongoing spiritual path.

Loving the life you live – this step is a lifelong project.

From this deep understanding of the structure of abusive relationships – and how to change your story creatively - you'll find the strength to reclaim your most precious possessions:

- Your confidence to be who you are.
- Your love of life

With practice you'll be able to turn your wounds into words. And your words into wisdom.

PART II
WOLF SPOTTING
Turning your gaze on the antagonist...

"...It is Christmas Day, the werewolves birthday, the door of the
solstice still wide enough to let them all slink through..."
Angela Carter

CHAPTER 14
A FIELD GUIDE TO WOLVES IN GENERAL

"...She did not know that the wolf was an evil animal, and therefore she was not afraid of him..."
  Jacob and Wilhelm Grimm

ROUGH GUIDE: HOW TO SPOT A WOLF

Wolves are notoriously difficult to spot.

They are shapeshifters – part human part wolf – werewolves. These men are often charming, charismatic, seductive and exciting.

As a collective they look like normal men (by that I mean kind-hearted souls who would never think of abusing a woman who loved him).

Wolves are good actors.

They know how to make an impression, how to make women notice them, how to fall into step with you on a narrow path through the woods.

In other words they know how to act like they're your friend.

AND THEY KNOW HOW TO MOVE THAT FRIENDSHIP INTO BED.

In this book I've referred to the wolf as 'he' but in some relationships he might be a 'she'.

Relationships where these power struggles and emotional abuse play out are mainly heterosexual but some of them take place in homosexual partnerships too.

I've had male readers write to me and tell me how they've suffered with a wolf woman in their bed.

However, to keep it simple I'm mainly talking about men of a certain kind.

You might be a gay man or woman in a relationship with a wolf of the same sex who has all the characteristics as described in this book.

Throughout the book I've referred to the wolf as 'he' to maintain clarity.

In essence, the wolf is playing the dominance game. Every relationship has a certain amount of power play involved in it and this is quite normal.

In a healthy relationship this balances out over time and each partner has their own 'sphere of authority' and feels respected as an individual.

However, as we've seen, this game of power gets out of hand when it turns toxic.

When this happens - your loving relationship makes you feel worthless and hopeless.

Whatever your sexual orientation, if you are in a relationship with a wolf, you'll be able to use the **DIOL** writing techniques in this book to help you recover.

Of course, no one is perfect.

But emotionally abusive wolves are often convinced they have a right to do behave badly.

They have a lot of history to support their attitudes towards women.

"... *throughout most of history* ***rape was considered a crime against men***..."

Ornstein

WHAT? RAPE – A CRIME AGAINST MEN? HOW COULD THAT BE? Well, that's because women were to blame for enticing men. They were guilty of being too sexually exciting.

They asked for it.

This explains why the girls who succeed in fairy tales (by success I mean, they get married to a high status male), tend to be passive, good and beautiful.

Both Sleeping Beauty and Snow White attracted their man while they were lying in a death-like coma. They didn't resist or complain or make a fuss when the prince comes along and... rapes them.

Sadly, these old school attitudes linger on in the minds of wolves.

They believe in fairy tales.

Women must be quiet, passive and still. Men can do what they like.

ALL WOLVES ARE THE SAME:

In some ways all wolves are the same.

Below you'll find the main characteristics they share.

After that, we'll look at the seven types of wolf. For now, here's a quick outline of every wolf's main attitudes.

His background matters but not in the way you might think. He is just as likely to have had a happy childhood as an unhappy one.

His attitudes and way of thinking are what makes him a wolf.

Don't feel sorry for him.

The way he thinks about women deep down is what makes him a wolf.

1. FIRSTLY, HE'S A MISOGYNIST: HERE'S A DICTIONARY DEFINITION: Misogyny; an unreasonable and uncontrollable dislike/distrust of women.

All wolves are misogynists however many times they open a door for you.

They see women as weak and not worthy of respect.

2. *HE'S A HEDONIST, BUT NOT IN A GOOD WAY:*

The wolf is a boy who just wants to have fun.

In his world - his happiness is more important than yours: Remember, the wolf is a misogynist with the old-fashioned idea that men should have power over women.

This is because they truly believe their lives are more important. Once again, not all of them are that obvious.

A wolf might talk like he's really 'right-on'; a liberal-minded, tolerant kind of guy who gives money to charity and treats his lady like a princess.

Well, even if he doesn't go that far; he'll certainly cover his true identity with care.

Ever heard the story about the wolf in sheep's clothing?

3. *HE'S A BULLY:* HE MIGHT NOT BE A RAPIST OR A WIFE-BEATER, but a true wolf will find a way to harm or hurt the women who love him.

He doesn't see anything wrong with his behaviour.

He's enjoying the power trip too much.

4. *HE'LL MAKE YOU HATE YOURSELF:* LET'S SAY YOU'VE MANAGED to crawl out of a relationship with a wolf. You're left with no self-confidence and feeling like you're worthless, ugly and your life is pointless.

If you're still with him, he regularly makes you feel this way. You hate yourself.

You might have considered suicide. Stop right there.

The things he says to you when he's having one of his tantrums are not true.

You're okay. You're a fallible, normal human being just like the rest of us.

5. **_ACCORDING TO HIM; IT'S ALL YOUR FAULT:_** THAT'S RIGHT. YOUR relationship difficulties are all down to you. He's the good one.

He does everything he can to please you and you just let him down time and time again.

Sounds familiar? He's a wolf.

Your inability to please him twenty-four seven is the greatest failing a human being could have. These ideas are harmful. It's subtle and sinister, and it breaks not only your heart, but your will too.

6. **_HE'S AN EXPERT IN PLAYING NICE:_** HE'S CAPABLE AT BEING lovely. That's why you fell in love with him in the first place. When he's not giving in to his wolf desire to destroy you, he's probably a wonderful, funny, sexy man.

That's why you're with him.

Contrary to his opinion, you are not stupid.

You're just really good at loving. Even when the object of your love is trying to destroy you.

7. **_IT'S UNLIKELY THAT HE'LL CHANGE:_** WHY WOULD HE? Remember, he's addicted to the power he feels in a relationship.

He's expecting a perfect princess.

He's constantly disappointed when a woman turns out to be a flawed human being just like anyone else.

He wants a 'living doll', an all-singing, all- dancing, ever-sexy worshipper of himself.

When you look into his past, you'll find that all his relationships follow roughly the same pattern.

8. **_HIS PAST RELATIONSHIPS ARE MURKY:_** HE'LL TELL YOU HOW

badly he's been treated by women in the past. If you listen carefully –
you'll hear that he uses abusive language to describe previous
partners.

He puts them down so much you're amazed he got out alive.

They might even have 'falsely' accused him of being abusive.

This is a warning sign.

A Field Guide to Wolf Personality Types

"They start with a killer first impression. Somehow they look a little
better than other people – more talented, more interesting, more
competent, more caring, more glamorous or just more fun.

Then, they're easy to talk to. They seem to understand you right
away, to know what you want. Even when you suspect smoke and
mirrors, you almost believe that what you think you see is what you'll
actually get..."

Albert J. Bernstein, Ph. D.

A wolf by any other name

Is still a wolf...

In this chapter we'll have a look at the seven main types of wolf.

Although they're all the same in the ways we've discussed – the way
they act out their negative feelings towards women differs.

The sinister Mr Death-by-a-Thousand-Cuts is a really good
deceiver.

You might find that no one who knows him will ever believe what
he's really been doing to you.

And the creepy Mr Sheep's-Clothing will also fool most of the
people, most of the time.

However, a wolf is a wolf is a wolf.

The first step towards finding out if he is one - was doing the abuse
checklists.

Five or more on both lists and you've got a problem.

If he's been physically abusive you don't even need the checklists to know that he's emotionally abusive too.

And even if he's never even pushed you out of the way on his way to a meeting of his other admirers - if you scored high on the abuse checklists - then he's a wolf.

IN MANY WAYS, GETTING A CLEAR VIEW OF WHICH WOLF GOT INTO your bed gives you the key.

It's the key to unlocking the guilt, anger, pain, fear and sadness you're holding inside.

You use the pen in your hand to explore what you find behind that door.

You're **Discovering your story** – by knowing the main characters.

And once you've got a clear focus – a good picture of who your wolf really is – you'll be ready for the final stage of discovering the fairy tale prison he's created for you.

Then you can start to **Imagine** how the story can end – in a way that suits you.

THE TROUBLE WITH ALL THAT ANGER

Then you can stop turning your anger inwards. The trouble is – **you've got a right to be angry.**

This was someone who said he loved you.

Someone you loved and trusted.

I know. It really hurts.

Turning anger inwards is what women usually do. This becomes self-destructive if left unchecked. Especially if you've lived through the trauma of emotional abuse.

There is nowhere for your anger to go. So it goes inside.

Anger turned inwards warps into depression.

Clinically defined or not – these low feelings can lead to self-harm. There are many ways a woman might self-harm, especially if she's dealing with the aftermath of emotional abuse.

She might use:

- Food, either overeating or under eating
- Guilt – constantly self-criticising
- Anxiety - constantly worrying over small things instead of taking on the real issues
- Drugs or alcohol to escape from her feelings.
- Cutting

YOUR IWW WILL PROTECT YOU...

Guess what though? Instead of turning anger inwards – you can put that stuff down on paper instead.

It won't harm you or anyone else to do this.

All those feelings, the ones you hardly dared to think about – write them down. It's fine.

Remember - your **IWW** won't tell you to write anything you can't handle.

Everything that comes out – comes out because you're ready. Rage if you like – rage upon the page. It won't hurt anyone. Instead - it'll be healing, cathartic and probably the most worthwhile thing you ever do.

After it's done, you can start **Imagining** a new ending to the story, a new life for you and your children if you have them. It's a step on the path to **Love.** Loving your life again. Living the life you love and loving the people who deserve it.

You might find it's both a shock and a relief to discover who you wolf really is.

A shock because you trusted him with your deepest secret self. And expected him to treat you with love and respect.

It's a relief because at last, you can finally understand what's been going on in his head.

After the years of confusion and pain, your relationship will make some kind of crazy sense. He wasn't who you thought he was.

IN FACT, YOU DIDN'T REALLY KNOW HIM AT ALL. THAT'S BECAUSE THE man you fell in love with is an illusion, a character he created to lure you in.

After I discovered the true character of the wolf in my bed – I still loved him.

Remember those hostages in Stockholm?

But the main thing was that I understood what had gone wrong.

I realised I wasn't to blame for making him unhappy. He had given me the job of making him unhappy.

Weird as that sounds, it's true.

Think about it. As a wolf - you believe that all women are inferior. So, how can a woman make you happy? It's just not possible.

A wolf despises all women and you're never going to be the exception.

You'll probably find that the wolf in your bed is a mixture of the types outlined below.

However, one main character type should stand out.

EXPLORE THIS CHARACTER TYPE IN THE QUICK WRITE AT THE END of this chapter.

Then you'll find your wolf-radar is tuned in much better. Also, the questionnaire will help you sort out which is his dominant type.

As you discover the true nature of the wolf in your bed, you're less likely to let another one take his place.

Once you've recovered from the trauma of emotional abuse, armed with this knowledge, you'll be able to take care of yourself.

With a pen in your hand for self-care, leaving the other hand free to take care of those closest to you.

Read the list in the following chapter through carefully – preferably more than once.

Afterwards, do the Quick Write and read over what comes out of your subconscious mind onto the page.

And if you can't quite decide, don't worry.

Do the exercise a couple of time. Because deep down, your **Inner Wise Woman** or **IWW** knows your wolf.

She knows exactly who he is – and what he is.

Read over the following seven characteristic wolf types more than once.

Be in touch with how you respond to each description.

Be aware of any feelings you have while reading. Think about how you would name these feelings.

You might feel: fear, anxiety, surprise, anger, uncertainty, resistance, hurt, recognition, sadness.

Or a mixture of all of them.

Or you might just feel numb – with a hint of recognition when you come across your wolf.

Your feelings are your instincts.

Your thoughts are your guide.

You're allowing yourself to heal.

CHAPTER 15
THE CHARACTERISTIC WOLVES:

I. **Mr Entitled:**

MR ENTITLED IS A SPOILED CHILD IN A MAN'S BODY.

He feels entitled to everything.

In a relationship that means basically that he's entitled to everything you can give him. And then some.

He's so good and wonderful – he keeps telling you this and at first you believe him.

He might be very successful at work and a leader of men. Everyone looks up to him. Including you.

But as soon as you stop finding him totally awesome every moment of his life – he's not happy.

He should be right at the centre of your life. He's the sun and you're a planet on an orbit of joy around him. If you get tired of this, he's angry. It means you're not meeting his needs.

He often blames you for all his problems. Even if they are nothing to do with the relationship.

After a while with this wolf - you will feel as though nothing you do is good enough. No matter how hard you try – you can't make him happy.

Criticism is his main weapon. It's his defining character trait.

Nasty, cutting comments about your shortcomings – all wrapped up in ironic, jokey little parcels. Or sometimes not.

It's as though Mr Entitled keeps an spreadsheet somewhere of everything you ever did wrong.

He's also got a column of all the good things he's done for you. However long ago they were.

Often, he likes to remind you of his generosity. And he wants gratitude. More and more of it.

Never stop the gratitude coming or you'll have to pay the price.

When he's in one of his moods he'll tell you how little you appreciate him – however much you try to make it clear it to him that do.

In other words, he ignores any of your grateful behaviour. Or any of the good times. He's too busy remembering what a bad girl you've been. He will punish you whenever he feels you've let him down – even if you don't know what you've done.

You feel like you're constantly skating on very thin ice.

At any moment, if you stop spinning in a way that pleases him – you'll fall through.

Your energy for the other parts of your life is draining away. As this relationship continues, your career will suffer first. Then your relationships with the other people you care about. Your children, family and friends.

If you ever try to discuss your own needs with him, he'll attack you by turning it back on you. Usually by – telling you how selfish you are.

Ah, the irony. It's ironic because one of his main characteristics is the habit of always twisting things round so the fault lands right back on you.

For example – in fact - he is the one who is selfish by expecting constant worship and gratitude from you. But when you try and discuss your emotions or problems suddenly it's all becomes about him. And how much you're letting him down.

2. Mr Know-it-All:

He's much more intelligent that you – at least that's what he believes.

And he's always on the moral high ground.

You on the other hand, are located somewhere in the swamps of stupidity and unethical behaviour below.

Because he's so much smarter and wiser than you - it's very important for him to tell you how to think.

You end up feeling like he's the professor and you're a very dim student.

He knows everything. Or thinks he does.

From the correct way to train your dog to how to book a holiday – and he knows how to do it best. In the end you'll find it hard to do all but the simplest everyday tasks. Even if you've spent your life before you were with him doing these things without a problem.

This is because he's ground down your confidence over time. You'll find that if you don't agree with him one hundred per cent, you're attacking him. He will turn this into the marathon task of getting your thinking straightened out.

It might take hours or days or weeks. But sooner or later you'll just have to agree with him.

He knows everything. You know nothing.

If you try to express an opinion of your own, even it's on a subject that you definitely know more about – you're in trouble.

How could you treat him so badly by having an opinion of your own? It's you of course, who is wrong.

Every time.

He'll find plenty wrong with your closest friends too.

They are weak or uncaring. Whatever faults he can find in them, he will.

He'll despise the people who care about you.

He's so much better than all of them.

You have to agree with him. It's too exhausting to have your own ideas. The whole world would be better off if he was in charge. And you need to think exactly the same way that he does. Otherwise, you're not only stupid, but also one of those horrible women who treat their men like equals.

Basically he just wants you to shut up unless you're agreeing with him.

3. Mr Death-by-a-Thousand-Cuts:

His mantra goes something like this: *smile as you slice*.

He knows how to push all your buttons and has a smirk on his face if you lose control.

He'll put you down as much as he feels he has a right to – but he'll do it in a quiet, chatty sort of way.

If insults were bullets he'd be using air gun pellets from a distance – over and over again.

This kind of slow, steady abuse acts like the sea wearing away a chalk cliff. And it can have the worst effect on you psychologically - worse than all the other methods of emotional abuse.

Because this kind of abuse is the hardest to talk about.

It's so confusing and well – hidden.

Did he really say that? This wolf enjoys using small cruelties – liberally sprinkled over everything you do together.

A woman in bed with this kind of wolf is the most likely to blame herself for their problems.

To discover she's been abused is so difficult to accept and yet crucial to her recovery. He's quiet but deadly – constantly cutting you with his little, tiny knife.

Worse still, he has no idea how mean he is. And neither do most of your friends.

No one understands why you get so angry and upset with him. Even your children might be mystified – and think there's something wrong with you instead.

He'll probably tell them you're crazy – on special outings without mum.

Finally, you have to agree with him.

His campaign has been successful.

You too end believing you've got some kind of mental illness.

Mr Death-by-a-Thousand-Cuts will make sure everyone knows how difficult and crazy you are. He'll complain about your difficult and crazy behaviour to all your friends behind your back. And then he'll come home and smile that smile at you. As he slices you up one more time.

His method is cruelty by stealth.

He'll invade your mind, your soul and wreck everything. He'll break you down, bit by subtle bit.

4. **Mr King-of-the-Control-Freaks:**

He's the only one who can run your life in an orderly manner.

This wolf will oversee his woman's life down to the smallest detail.

He will even train your children to spy on you. His capacity for paranoia and jealousy is outstanding.

He doesn't like any other man talking to you or even looking at you. And he hates it if you work closely with men. If that's the case, he's likely to put a stop to your career.

After all, a woman should be looking after her man. She should be close to her man. She doesn't need anyone else.

He believes that there's only one person in whole wide world you should be close to and that's him.

Eventually, he's in control of every part of your life. If he wasn't of course, you'd get it all wrong.

There's nothing wrong with this in his eyes because he only does it because he loves you.

He's also revolted by you but somehow this makes sense to him.

Everything has to be perfect in his world.

The way you prepare his food or clean the house or make the beds – all have to be done according to his exact instructions. You'll be told what to wear, what to read and what to say.

A mark on the car will send him into a rage and his rages are your job to sort out.

He's not responsible for the imperfections of his life. You are.

Even if this wolf is driving you mad – take care if you ever try to leave him.

He's the kind of wolf who might turn violent.

If you feel threatened and imprisoned by this type of wolf your escape plan needs to be good.

Get help.

5. Mr Sheep's-Clothing:

Ah, he's a tricky one and no mistake. He's so thoughtful and kind.

He doesn't do all that macho, alpha male stuff. In fact, he's totally in touch with his feminine side. Good grief, he'll even watch romantic comedies with you and cry...

He's helpful and kind when he isn't being abusive. So on the surface he's the perfect man. But it's a cover.

Mr Sheep's-Clothing is as cunning and manipulative as he is capable of being kind to the elderly.

He opens up about his emotions.

He'll discuss the importance of women's issues and human rights.

He's probably into green issues too and feels connected to the natural world.

Oh my, how he loves animals and sunsets and weeps at sad songs about dying dogs.

It's so wonderful to find a man like this. Well, it would be if he was the real thing.

And if you try to talk about what's really going on in this relationship – all your friends just shrug it off.

How can he be a problem – he cries every time he watches *The Sound of Music?*

They think you're imagining it – and in that way he's a bit like Mr Death- by-a-Thousand-Cuts.

But this wolf is different. His main problem is that you keep on hurting his feelings.

And boy, does he have a lot of feelings for you to accidentally step on.

The thing is – he's not interested in your feelings. If you've got a problem, it's simply not as deeply felt as his.

He's got to get back onto the subject of his emotional life as quickly as possible.

Truth is, underneath the crying and musical theatre - there's a mean streak in him ten miles wide – but you seem to be the only one who gets to see it.

He can also be quite threatening – pushing or shoving you around during an argument.

But this aggression will be your fault.

You've wound him up deliberately and made him behave badly. During the good times you'll have opened up to him about your fears and desires.

When he's abusing you, this is what he'll use against you. He's like a New Age psychoanalyst trying a method of extreme therapy on you.

He knows how you think and likes to twist it around so you're the crazy one.

When you try to complain, he likes to point out that he's not like most men. You should appreciate who he is and put his feelings first every time.

Poor him. He's so very, very sensitive.

And don't ever dare forget that.

He's convinced he's the fragile, sensitive one.

He might be struggling with addiction. Or a long-standing mental illness. In which case, you should be supporting him. All the time.

Whatever he does. Whatever he says.

Exhausted?

You will be.

6. Mr Smooth:

He's a sex god and no mistake.

When you first get together it was most likely a time of sexual awakening for you.

He adores you and worships your body.

He's probably quite handsome too, so you feel great that a man like this has fallen in love with you as much as you've fallen for him.

But. It doesn't take too long for his attention to stray.

Not long after all that intensity he's not so enthusiastic about having sex with you anymore.

In fact, your sex life might become routine, dare I say it dull. For you at least.

He seems to be okay though.

Most women catch his eye. Your sister or your best friend, a barmaid or his new PA, there are no off- limits for this wolf. He's in a relationship with you and that's fine – he wanted it so much at the beginning.

But he doesn't want to be tied down.

Besides, he can't help it if other women like to be around him.

To keep his attention, you might start to experiment with different sexual activities.

You might even go beyond your comfort zone during this time. However, other women still seem to be more exciting to him than you.

He likes the company of women – and what's wrong with that?

This wolf enjoys the drama of life at arm's length.

He winds up the different women in his life, turning them against each other.

This can often result in anger flaring up between women – and he'll be on the side-lines innocently watching.

Like all wolves, he loves to talk about how women have let him down in the past.

He uses vile language when he does this. But he's great at making you feel like you're the one he really loves. He's probably saying this to your best friend too.

Sometimes he'll tell you he needs you.

He can't live without you. You're his soul mate.

But when he's in one of his abusive moods he'll hardly speak to you.

He'll turn his back on you when you take off your clothes – the one thing that used to please him.

He'll be verbally abusive, often about your body or your attitudes to sex.

And even if he's not actually sleeping with other women, he's always flirting. This is just as harmful and unkind in the long run.

If you feel sorry for him, you might think he's a sex addict. He's not.

He just likes to play around with women because it's fun to see their reactions.

He doesn't care if it hurts them or their children.

He's having fun and that's all that counts.

7. Mr Macho:

He's the most likely to be physically violent as well as emotionally abusive.

He's strong and intimidating with everyone – not just you. Sometimes he's your protector – especially at the beginning – just like all wolves.

He'll make you feel special.

You can hide behind him and feel completely safe.

He puts his lovely big arms around you and at last you're home.

No one would dare give you any trouble while you're with him. After all, he knows how to take care of business. And he's promised to take care of you.

But. It doesn't take long for him to show his other side.

He definitely thinks he's superior to women and looks down on you from a great bulging height. The only thing he respects is physical strength and as woman, you'll hardly have enough of that to impress him. He's got no time for soppiness.

Above all, he won't walk away from a fight. People might think he's gay if he did. He thinks being homosexual is as bad as being a woman.

So, once he's got in your bed and in your heart and he starts showing his true colours – well, you feel more and more that you need to be protected *from* him.

He's like the stereotype of what a real man should be.

His upbringing was tough and he's tough and he doesn't have much time for weaklings. Grrrr.

Don't get me wrong, there are plenty of 'gentle giants' out there who look or act like macho men but are in fact, pussy cats.

They might be all tattooed muscle and rugby on a Saturday, but don't get them confused with Mr Macho the wolf.

To the macho wolf, his masculinity is all that matters to him. All that feminine stuff is just pathetic.

Women need to know their place, and if it takes the odd slap to show you who's boss – then there you go. That's life mate.

The worst thing is a 'gobby' or mouthy woman.

A woman with strong opinions? She's asking for it anyway. Blah blah blah.

If you've been in love with this wolf, you know all his excuses.

In his extreme form, this wolf will just make you believe he's going to kill you – even if he hasn't actually harmed you yet. This version of Mr Macho might not be a big man either – in fact he might be quite small and weedy.

But he's really, really scary when he's in the wrong mood. That's when he'll make the kind of threatening statements that cause terror in your heart.

He might threaten to harm you.

Or make it clear that bad things will happen to you or your children.

There is an intelligent mad scientist version of Mr Macho.

He likes to see you live with the festering fear.

This is because he owns you – body, mind and soul.

Deep down he thinks you're the evil one. He gets off on seeing how afraid you are of him.

These kinds of wolves are the most dangerous of all.

Let me repeat that. ***These wolves are the most dangerous of all***. If he threatens to kill you or make bad things happen to you – he probably will.

And this wolf is the most likely to harm the children too.

If that what it takes to frighten you.

Please, please get help if this is your wolf. You need to get away.

QUICK WRITE

Find a quiet place and write this question down at the top of the page of your notebook?

Tell me who my wolf is?

Know that your IWW will know.

Let her speak.

Freewrite – don't think.

If she wants to add some characteristics to the above outline sketches of wolves, let her.

Give yourself 10 minutes writing time.

Afterwards read it back.

Is he a mixture?

Is he clearly one kind of wolf most of the time?

Is he dangerous?

They all are all harmful emotionally - but if he's likely to cause physical harm then you need to sort out that issue out first.

Do you need to ring a helpline?

Ask your IWW if you're not sure.

If there is no clear way that your wolf acts out – ask the main question again.

Tell me who my wolf is?

Don't worry if you still can't define him.

The questionnaire will help you find his dominant characteristic.

PART III

FAIRY TALES YOU WANT TO ESCAPE FROM

"Aha! Little Red Riding Hood!" says the Big Bad Wolf, upon finding the girl in the woods. "Now I'm going to take off your little red cape, lift up your little red skirt, pull down your little red panties and fuck your brains out!"

Ornstein

CHAPTER 16
A WOLF TRAPS YOU IN HIS FAIRY TALE WORLD

"...I always felt and still feel that fairy tales have an emotional truth that is so deep that there are few things that really rival them..." *(Alice Hoffman)*

HE TOOK YOU INTO HIS WORLD...

Remember the fairy ring?

When you fell in love with your wolf, he took you into his world.

This world is full of nightmares and illusion.

Here – he can treat you however he wants. He can run a campaign of verbal and emotional abuse to gain power over you.

He can destroy your self-confidence and wear you down.

Like a spoiled child, all he ever wanted was a fairy princess to play with.

He's made it quite clear what the number one rule is. *It's your fault if you're confused and upset by his behaviour.*

What follows next are seven fairy tales. Read through them carefully. Some of them you may know – but they might be different versions from the ones you heard as a child. Some might be new, but they're old, old stories and they hold a grain of truth about toxic love inside them.

Read them and while you read – notice how you feel. **Observe** these feelings. Reflect on them. Observation of your own emotions is one of your main recovery tools. Writing will increase your connection to these buried feelings. Through writing you'll get back in touch with the instinctive, intuitive part of yourself.

And once you've re-connected with this part – your IWW - you'll discovery which dark fairy tale you've been trapped inside.

Don't worry if the tales don't seem to have any relevance to your own life. Your IWW will do the hard work. She'll process the stories. She'll know where you've been – and how to get you out of there. You can use your writing as a ladder back to the real world. Back to the life you love.

Because your IWW is a part of you that lives in your subconscious mind – she understands images, symbols and dream-like language better than your waking self. She can interpret what is going on in the stories. But just to make it easier – I've included a list of symbols to pay attention to – at the end of each story. I've also outlined a similar story – set in the here and now. Just to give you an idea of how this type of story would looks in a real-world setting. And although these modern fairy tales are all works of fiction, each of them is a fictional take on a real relationship.

Fairy tales are like very strange dreams. The talking animals, canni-balism, shape-shifters, magic, kings, fairies and princesses – are more than a little surreal.

Your IWW is at home here.

This is her territory. She can work with this stuff. These stories will later become your rough guide to understanding the role you played in your wolf's game. But the world of his story was *not your world*. Later, when you've completed the questionnaire and **Discovered** which story most closely matches your own nightmare of abuse, you can **Imagine** a new ending. Once you've cleared out the debris of all the negative things your wolf made you believe about yourself – you can start **Observing** your emotions and watch them grow more positive.

Then you can write your way home to a life you **Love**.

CHAPTER 17
THE RED SHOES

O nce upon a time, there was an orphan girl called Karen. Her short life had been full of poverty, hunger, sadness and loneliness.

However, as she blossomed into a beautiful young woman she was adopted by a rich old woman.

The old woman loved to indulge the wild-hearted Karen. When Karen saw a pair of red silk Moroccan shoes, the old woman bought them for her.

Karen, knowing that no on one would approve if she wore anything red to church, could not resist putting them on one Sunday morning.

As she passed through the lych-gate (the archway through which the dead are brought to be buried) on her way to church, she saw a man.

He was a soldier with a pointed beard.

He looked at her feet and smiled.

'What pretty dancing shoes,' he said, stroking the red silk with his fingers.

'Thank you,' Karen said, blushing despite herself.

Karen started to dance for him. She danced until she was breathless but she could not stop. She danced through the dark night.

The shoes took her through a forest of thorns till she was torn and bleeding.

Then she thought she saw what looked like an angel by the path - his face was deathly pale and he reminded her of the soldier at the gate.

He said to her: 'You will dance until you are pale and cold, till your skin shrivels and you are a skeleton.'

She danced to the executioner's house and begged him to cut off her feet with the red shoes. So he did, with one blow of his axe, he chopped off both her feet.

But the shoes danced away with the little feet inside them. They danced across the fields into the deep forest. She had to follow them.

Soon, the hangman carved her a pair of wooden feet and some crutches. She hobbled after the red shoes. And wherever she went the red shoes were dancing before her, and she could find no rest and no mercy.

At last her skin shrivelled until she lost her beauty and she was nothing more than a crippled skeleton forever limping after her dancing feet.

At last, death claimed her. And her soul flew to Heaven where no one asked after the Red Shoes.

THE END

DID YOU DANCE FOR YOUR WOLF?

Have you ever felt you were performing for a wolf that was never satisfied? When you give it your best shot and it's never enough - what do you do?

If this is your story then you'll be with a wolf that raises the stakes all the time.

It takes more and more to satisfy him.

In the story of the Red Shoes, Karen keeps on dancing even though her feet bleed.

She can't eat, she can't sleep and finally, she dances herself to death.

The soldier/angel/devil at the lych-gate likes the shoes. He encourages her to dance. So does the soldier but not in a good way.

Are the soldier and the devil the same man dressed up differently?

If this wolf was in your bed you'll know the answer. One minute he was an angel and the next... well. He was a wolf.

In this story it's all Karen's fault because she wore red. And what's so bad about the colour red?

Red is one of the symbols we'll look at later one.

Meanwhile, ask yourself this question – what is the theme of this story?

IT'S A TALE OF OBSESSION.

Yes, it's about passion and obsession.

To begin with, Karen is a passionate woman. We know that because she loves her red silk shoes. She can't wait to wear them.

On the surface, this appears to be a shallow desire.

But shoes are more than just shoes – in the fairy-tale, dream-like, symbolic world at least.

WALKING IN YOUR OWN SHOES

Ever heard the saying 'to know a person you must walk in their shoes...'? In other words, you'll understand someone better if you see the world from their point of view, by walking with them for a while.

Shoes are a symbol of your connection to the earth.

They indicate how grounded you are in daily life. If you're 'in touch with the earth' then you're really living each moment.

Also, because you walk about in shoes they symbolise your *direction* in life.

In a healthy relationship each partner chooses a career, a direction, a way to express who they are through work.

They each support that choice in the other person. Together, a couple plans for the future.

This means they work towards the realisation of their dreams. To love someone is to respect their autonomy and that includes career choices.

At first the wolf at the lych-gate (he's a soldier in the story, but for our purposes we'll refer to him as a wolf), admires Karen's shoes. He compliments her. He likes the shoes and her exciting, unusual choice of direction by wearing them to church.

She's a rebel. She's daring to go her own way and she's walking in a new direction. As we saw earlier all wolves appear to be angels at the beginning of a relationship.

In this story the wolf wins Karen's trust by seeming to agree with her resolve to live on her own terms. But when he touches her shoes her life spins out of control.

His touch casts an evil spell on the shoes. Symbolically he's taken control of her direction in life. Then he sits back and watches her dance herself to death.

Karen is helpless.

Even when she cuts herself off from the direction she chose by slicing off her own feet, the shoes dance in front of her. She's lost in her obsession, unable to break away.

Her life is out of control.

The wonderful dance of her existence transforms into a life of horror. This makes even more sense if you remember that glass slipper in another story.

Lovely shoes in folk tales are a sign of beauty, but by the end of this story, Karen is disfigured. She's a footless skeleton obsessed with dancing.

She loses both her inner and outer beauty. This makes it much easier for the wolf to despise her.

If this is your story you'll have dedicated your life to pleasing the wolf. But when the emotional abuse continues long-term, you'll become exhausted.

Having lost your sparkle, the brightness that attracted him at the beginning he'll find it easier and easier to show you that you disgust him.

It's also worth remembering that shoes are often a symbol of sexuality.

Karen's open and free expression of her sexual needs is turned against her. There is a deep-rooted hint in this story of sexual coercion – another wolf trait.

And symbols of sex bring us neatly to the colour red...

THE COLOUR RED.

Red is the colour of blood, heat, fire, anger, sexuality, danger, lust and temptation.

These are all the dazzling qualities of a woman who loves life. Karen isn't afraid to explore everything - including love and sex. She's enthusiastic and fun-loving.

She's free and easy-going. This will both irritate and attract a certain kind of wolf more than anything else in a woman.

If you look at her one way, she's a feisty chick with a big heart.

But if you look at her from the point of view of a certain kind of wolf – she's a Scarlet woman who needs to be taught a lesson. She's a whore if she likes sex, and a bitch if she doesn't.

It's a lose-lose situation.

If you've lived out this fairy tale, you'll start your love affair feeling really special.

Your wolf will admire your joy, your vitality and your gutsy approach. He'll encourage you to dazzle him. Endless dancing is a great metaphor for the exhausting performance the wolf will demand of you.

At first he'll make you feel warm and sexy. He'll love and admire your 'Red Shoes' – your life force in other words. But after a while, he'll slip into the cycle of emotional abuse as his admiration of your sparkling self will turn into something more like hatred.

Every now and then he'll throw you a crumb of love – just like the old days.

So you keep on dancing, hoping to make everything right again. But over time your dance of joy becomes a desperate struggle.

In the end, he condemns you for everything he used to love about you. But by then it's too late.

You're dancing out of fear.

When Karen chops off her own feet and becomes crippled – she's effectively losing an important part of who she is. Without feet she can't dance, she's lost direction and most importantly she's lost all her confidence.

Also, she finds it almost impossible to run away from him. He's controlling her fate, her direction in life by controlling her shoes.

He watches impassively as she staggers onwards, searching for a way back to the safety of her own soul – as symbolised by the church.

A Wolf in Angel's Clothing...

When Karen meets what she thinks is angel at the side of the road she thinks she's found a friend.

However, just like the wolf – the angel is determined to punish her for wearing the Red Shoes.

In Christian terms, angels were always male and their main job was to deliver messages from God. In this story it seems at first glance that Karen's punishment far outweighs her sin.

To be condemned to dance to death for wearing unsuitable shoes feels harsh in the extreme. Perhaps if a male, misogynistic god wanted to put women in their place – then this angel would indeed be his messenger.

However, at the end, Karen goes to heaven, so we know her God has not condemned her.

The angel she glimpses could be seen as an indication of the duel nature of all abusive men.

He can be so loving, tender, angelic.

And he can be so cruel.

The angel's message to Karen is that she'll dance until:

'... your skin shrivels and you are a skeleton...'

In other words - you'll dance until you die.

However, it makes more sense when we think about what those shoes really mean symbolically. Because fairy tales have a dream-like quality symbolic meaning is everything.

So, if the shoes indicate that Karen is a woman with a clear direction or career, someone who knows what she wants and is prepared to get it and she's got no inhibitions about her sexuality, it becomes clear that she's a threat.

What is so threatening about a woman who knows what she wants out of life?

Well, the problem is this.

It's the main characteristic stopping a man having power over her.

If she's a strong career woman who is also attractive and feisty, she's going to have her own mind. Ah, you might say: but we've come such a long way in terms of women's equality and human rights.

Perhaps we have on paper and in legislation.

Unfortunately, certain types of wolves still don't appreciate that this is a good thing.

Especially the critical wolf.

In his world the perfect woman is a stereotype of wifely duty and demure behaviour. He might be attracted to her initially but he still despises her deep down for her vision and talent.

Once he's got into her bed, he does everything he can to destroy her career and lust for life.

He punishes her sexual nature any way he can.

He's envious of her and at the same time he's really angry that she's so uppity and confident. By the time he's finished with her she's lost her confidence and her career is in tatters.

Worst of all, her inner Self is shrivelled and skeletal.

A MODERN-DAY TALE OF THE RED SHOES

Here's an example of how the Red Shoes might play out in a street near you:

Once upon a time there was woman who loved to bake.

Her name was Karen and she'd had a difficult life but she'd overcome her past and was building a little business making cakes for celebrations.

She had lots of friends, a nice little rented cottage and a red car.

When she met Keith on one of her cake-baking courses he raved about her cakes and told her how talented she was. It was love at first sight and they were soon living together.

Their wedding day was wonderful and the centrepiece was a beautiful cake made by Karen. She was a bit hurt that he criticised the cake. It was too sweet. Too much chocolate and not enough raisins.

For her part, she spent the next few months perfecting the recipe, along with all her others, but Keith had begun to lose interest in eating the results.

From then on she baked and baked and tried to make him happy - but Keith had other things on his mind. And his needs loomed over her life.

First of all, it was important to him that Karen always came with him on his business trips away. She lost a lot of customers because she didn't have as much time to bake as she needed.

She baked whenever she could but it was exhausting.

The late nights began to annoy Keith. He needed more sex and she was always too busy.

Also, he made it clear he didn't like his kitchen cluttered up with her cake-making stuff.

After a couple of years he finally told her how unhappy her obsession with cakes was making him. Sure, he liked to cook too, but nothing as frivolous as cakes.

He explained to Karen that her curvy figure which had once entranced him was putting him off her. He called her horrible names. He told her she was growing fat and ugly and would probably die of heart disease due to all that cholesterol.

By now, Karen was so unhappy she ate more cakes than she sold.

Keith didn't want to take her on business trips anymore and she couldn't keep up payments on her lovely red car.

Shut inside the house day after day she baked and baked and baked hoping to re-create the recipe that had once made Keith so happy.

One day, with a sigh of despair, Karen fell to the floor weeping and stayed there all night unable to move.

Her business had failed, her cakes were all wrong, she'd lost all her friends and her marriage was a disaster.

The next day Keith moved out without leaving a forwarding address.

THE END

Quick Write:

In your notebook write for 5 minutes.

Use this question as a prompt:

What is passion?

Let your **IWW** guide your pen.

Have you ever fallen in love too quickly?

Have you ever felt bad about enjoying your own body?

Have you ever found a partner criticising your chosen career?

Are you fiery and passionate by nature but have lost contact with this side of yourself?

Are you constantly exhausted, or were you when you were in a toxic relationship?

CHAPTER 18
SLEEPING BEAUTY OR SUN, MOON AND TALIA...

S un, Moon, and Talia (Sole, Luna, e Talia) is an Italian literary tale written down by Giambattista Basile in 1643. Charles Perrault retold this fairy tale in 1697 as Sleeping Beauty.

AFTER THE BIRTH OF A GREAT LORD'S DAUGHTER, TALIA, WISE MEN AND astrologers cast the child's horoscope and told the lord that Talia would be later endangered by a splinter of flax.

To protect his daughter, the father commands that no flax would ever be brought into his house.

Years later, Talia sees an old woman spinning flax on a spindle.

She asks the woman if she can stretch the flax herself, but as soon as she begins to spin, a splinter of flax goes under her fingernail, and she drops to the ground, apparently dead.

Unable to stand the thought of burying his child, the lord puts Talia in one of his country estates.

Some years later, a king, hunting in nearby woods, follows his falcon into the house.

He finds Talia, tries unsuccessfully to wake her up, and rapes her.

Afterwards, he leaves the girl on the bed and returns to his own city.

Still deep in sleep, she gives birth to twins (a boy and a girl). One day, the boy cannot find his mother's breast; and instead he begins to suck on Talia's finger and draws the flax splinter out.

Talia awakens immediately. She names her children, "Sun" and "Moon", and lives with them in the house.

The king returns and finds Talia is awake – and a mother of twins.

However, he is already married so he goes away again.

He calls out the names of Talia, Sun and Moon in his sleep, and the queen hears him. She forces the king's secretary to tell all and, with a forged message, brings the children to court.

She orders the cook to kill the children and serve them to the king. The cook hides them and cooks two lambs. The queen taunts the king while he eats.

Then the queen has Talia brought to court. She commands that a huge fire be lit in the courtyard, and that Talia be thrown into the flames.

Talia asks to take off her fine garments first. The queen agrees. Talia undresses and utters screams of grief with each piece of clothing.

The king hears Talia's screams. His wife tells him that Talia would be burned and that he had unknowingly eaten his own children.

The king commands that his wife, his secretary, and the cook be thrown into the fire instead. The cook explains how he had saved Sun and Moon. The king and Talia marry; and the cook is rewarded with the title of royal chamberlain.

The last line of the fairy tale – its moral – is as follows: "Lucky people, so 'tis said, He who has luck may go to bed, And bliss will rain upon his head."

The End

DID HE LIKE YOU BEST WHEN YOU WERE ASLEEP?

Well, perhaps not fast asleep – but quiet and passive.

This is because if you've lived through this story then your wolf will be the kind who only wants a woman if she shuts up and agrees with him.

The theme of this story is compliance or total submission.

A comatose woman is raped.

She bears children to the rapist and then marries him.

Lucky man.

Sun, Moon and Talia is probably the oldest version of Sleeping Beauty.

Notice that the king falls in love with Talia when he thinks she's not just sleeping but *dead*. Falling in love might be the wrong expression. He's a necrophiliac.

Hmm. Nice guy.

Even if your wolf would never have sex with you when you were asleep, he may have wanted a passive, submissive woman.

Above all, this story is about female obedience.

LET'S EXPLORE THIS STORY A BIT MORE. IN IT, TALIA'S COMA IS A symbolic state of mind.

She's compliant and silent about the king's lack of respect for her.

Symbolically, there are many different ways to be 'asleep'. In this fairy tale the king falls in love not with Talia – but with the idea of an obedient or if you like - 'dead' woman.

A 'DEAD' WOMAN IS VERY QUIET

Is your wolf only happy when he's teaching you how to behave?

Is he an expert on everything?

How well does he deal with anyone whose opinions are different from his?

Answer these questions to see whether your wolf ever cast you as Talia.

- If your wolf was always correcting your behaviour – for your own good
- If he was the fount of all knowledge – this was your story, especially if...
- It was never a good idea to have an opinion of your own on anything

- And he hated everyone who didn't think the same way as him.

SLEEPING BEAUTY SHOULD REALLY BE CALLED DEAD BEAUTY.

She's as inanimate as one of those rubber sex dolls. She's a Living Doll – the one Cliff Richard sang a love song about in the twentieth century. I always found that song kind of creepy.

Talia is the kind of woman who dares not have a thought in her head unless it's one she's been told she can have.

Ever heard of the Stepford Wives? They were the perfect women apparently.

They wore flowery dresses, cooked delicious food and never refused sex. They were robots – I think – I don't remember the story that well. I know the film scared the hell out of me when I saw it.

The thing about a dead person, someone dead inside anyway, is that she's very quiet. A dead woman doesn't argue or disagree or have opinions. She doesn't refuse sex. She's as good as gold.

If this was your main story your wolf will be like a strict father figure and you'll be his little girl. When you're good he's satisfied. But no one is good all the time unless they're a robot. So you'll fail him of course. Because you're not dead.

In Sun, Moon and Talia the rapist king is married when he meets Beauty. After his wife hears about Talia and her children, she takes revenge and the guilt is loaded onto her.

Remember how rape used to be considered a crime against a man?

Beauty had asked for it by being so beautiful.

It wasn't his fault.

However, let's look at the king's wife from a different angle. What if she's a symbol of the king's own feminine side? The psychologist Jung thought that everyone's personality is a mixture of male and female elements. In a man, the feminine part was called the 'Anima'.

This gives us an interesting insight into...

THE KING'S FEMININE SIDE

This is the key to knowing why this wolf behaves the way he does.

Because if the king or wolf or rapist despises all women it makes sense that he'll hate his own feminine side too.

The fluid, caring, nurturing side of him will be neglected, repressed and very, very angry.

His Anima, angry and repressed, is the part of him who might well try and serve up his children as lunch. She's been pushed aside too long.

She's had no chance to develop and she's to blame for everything. He despises this part of himself as much as he despises you.

But how does this help us understand the story?

Well, it means **the king always has to have a woman to blame.** He can blame her for everything that goes wrong in his life.

He has to punish her too.

In his warped mind – women can never make good decisions.

IN HIS EYES - WOMEN ARE STUPID AND WRONG ABOUT EVERYTHING. Did the wolf in your bed see you this way?

If this is your story then you've been living with a Perfectionist. Above all - the king is a perfectionist.

This means that he'll only ever love you when you're passive, submissive, quiet and hardly moving. He sees you as a child who should be seen and not heard.

A MODERN-DAY TALE OF SUN, MOON AND TALIA

Here's an example of how the Sun, Moon and Talia might play out in a street near you:

Once upon a time there was a woman called Talia who worked as a school secretary.

The headmaster, Richard King, was a serious man. Handsome too, and dedicated to his school and his profession. He was also married.

A few evenings a week he'd chat to Talia about how hard his life was. His wife was a terrible burden. He described her as a crazy, jealous bitch. She made him so awfully unhappy.

Talia listened carefully. She was a good listener. She felt sorry for Mr King.

Mr King was such a wonderful head teacher.

He made all the children wear proper uniforms. He introduced after-school clubs and a strict code of discipline. Talia thought he deserved better in his private life. She started sleeping with Mr King to make him happy.

And for a while he was happy with her.

He told her he loved her but he couldn't leave his wife. She might kill herself – she was a mad cow. Poor him.

However, one day he turned up at Talia's house in a terrible state. According to him, his horrible bitch of a wife had left him without saying a word. He had nowhere else to go.

He divorced the wife and married Talia without further ado.

Talia soon discovered how important it was to do everything properly.

Richard King knew exactly how to run a home as well as a school. Talia couldn't think how she ever managed on her own.

At first she tried to make helpful suggestions.

She'd always been good with computers but her ideas, as it turned out, were all wrong. Mr King knew the right way to use the damn things.

He also knew how to cook, clean, keep accounts and run a car properly. Oh dear, Talia had been doing it all wrong for years.

In the end, she gave up thinking her own thoughts and just agreed with him.

She got rid of the cat because it was a health hazard. She also started suffering from insomnia. Every night she lay awake worrying she might have left the lights on, or the front door unlocked, or the cups unwashed. All these things would send Mr King into a mood.

He called her vile names, used the sort of language he would never have tolerated at work.

But Talia believed she deserved it. She had so much to learn and he was the only one who could teach her.

She was forty-three.

After a few years, Talia felt like she was invisible. She was so tired she could hardly think straight. She worked hard all day, then came home and scrubbed and cooked and made sure everything was just the way Mr King liked it.

She often found herself weeping on the spotless bathroom floor at three o'clock in the morning.

One day, she vowed, she'd do things properly. She'd stop making stupid mistakes and upsetting her husband. And Mr King would be as pleased with her as he was in their first few months together. She'd never been so wretched in her whole life. And it was all her own fault.

She was so unworthy of Mr King's love, she felt as though she was becoming invisible.

QUICK WRITE:

Find a quiet place you like to write in.
Use this question as a prompt:
What is perfection?
As always, let your IWW take charge.
Don't think, just let the words come.
Write for 5 minutes.

CHAPTER 19
HANS MY HEDGEHOG

H ans my Hedgehog was collected by the brothers Grimm and was published in 1819.

A WEALTHY BUT CHILDLESS MERCHANT WISHES HE HAD A CHILD, EVEN A hedgehog, and comes home to find that his wife has given birth to a baby boy that is a hedgehog from the waist up.

After eight years, the merchant goes to a fair and asks everyone in the household what they want.

Hans My Hedgehog asks for bagpipes, and when he receives them, asks his father to have shoes made for the cockerel so he can ride off to seek his fortune.

When he gets them, he goes off into the woods and watches over his donkeys and pigs.

A king, lost in the woods, hears him playing the bagpipes, and Hans My Hedgehog promises to show him the way home in return for whatever first meets him when he returns.

The king promises, but, realizing that Hans My Hedgehog cannot read, writes down instead that Hans My Hedgehog should receive nothing, which he is glad of when he returns and it is his daughter; she is glad of it, too.

A second king is also lost, and he doesn't write down the promise, and his daughter, on hearing of it, gives her promise that she will obey.

In time, Hans My Hedgehog goes to claim his promises.

The first king attempts to withhold his daughter, but Hans forces him to yield her, and then takes her off, forces her to take off her clothing, pierces her all over until she bleeds, and sends her back to her father.

The second king agrees to the marriage. The princess holds herself bound by her promise, and Hans My Hedgehog promises her that his prickles will not harm her.

Then he tells the king on their wedding night, he should build a big fire so that when Hans takes off his hedgehog coat, he should have four servants burn it.

They do this, and Hans My Hedgehog becomes a handsome young man.

The End

THIS IS A TALE OF RETRIBUTION, ANGER AND PAIN

Hans My Hedgehog expects to get everything he asks for. He's been spoiled rotten by his father.

So, when the first King tries to trick Hans, Hans takes it out on the king's daughter. That's the kind of retribution which doesn't make any sense to anyone except Hans.

But what's ever weirder is that no one seems to question what Hans My Hedgehog does to the woman whose skin he pierces.

Why does Hans get away with this kind of behaviour?

Two reasons.

One, it's a fairy tale and of course, in the surreal world of the fairy tale the rules are upside down.

Hans seems to think that the way he treats the first woman is okay. He distrusts and despises women. But he believes they should give themselves to him if he desires them.

So he'll hurt any woman who displeases him.

Secondly, Hans is a handsome young man. Underneath his rough, prickly exterior – he's gorgeous. And in his world, this makes up for everything.

He deserves the adoration of the second king's daughter because, according to his ego, he's so good looking anyone would fall in love with him.

Hans is not a deep man.

He's also adept at pretending to be nice. No one sees him scratching the skin of the first woman until she bleeds. He does these things in private.

This is like the reverse of a wolf in sheep's clothing.

Hans is a dangerous animal on the outside but on the inside he really believes he's wonderful. Hans suffers from a form of extreme self-esteem.

I'm still worried about what it must be like to live with him. He could turn back into a hedgehog any time.

SHAPESHIFTERS TURN UP IN EVERY CULTURE…

Humans turning into animals are a popular and universal symbol in tales, myths and legends from around the world. From werewolves to swans, humans get in touch with their animal side by becoming one of them.

Sometimes the full moon sets them off, and sometimes they get stuck in their animal 'skin' because they start to think like the creature they've become forgetting what it is to be human.

Hans My Hedgehog is selfish to the core.

He doesn't reveal his human side until he's in danger of losing the woman he tricked into marrying him.

It makes you wonder how long he can keep up his handsome look. Who is the real Hans?

I'm guessing he quite likes being a hedgehog, riding around on a cock playing his bagpipes!

SAVING FACE

The face we present to the world is very important.

Healthy people try and live up to their best characteristics. If your best face is a caring, funny, sincere one that's who you'd like to really be. And you strive to become that person as much as possible.

This is what psychologists call an 'integrated personality'. You know your other, less likeable 'faces' but you try to be the best you can.

Similarly, a healthy relationship is one where both partners are being authentic – keeping it real with each other.

This is how we should love and be loved.

By giving the best of ourselves as much as we can. And being honest.

Hans My Hedgehog is not honest to himself. He thinks he's a good looking guy with nothing to be ashamed of. Even when he's tortured a woman for no reason.

By lying to himself, he's lying to everyone around him.

- Does your wolf tell you how wonderful he is at every opportunity?
- Does he control every aspect of your life – but without it being obvious to outsiders?
- Does he act like a caring person when you're with other people?
- Does he complain about you behind your back?
- Does he prick you constantly with sarcastic comments?
- Do you fear he might turn violent one day?

IF THE WOLF IN YOUR BED HAS A STARK CONTRAST BETWEEN HIS public face and the private one he shows to you – the abusive face – then this is your story.

THE EFFECTS OF LONG-TERM SMALL CRUELTIES...

Perhaps you know exactly what I mean by this. Even if you think you don't, it's worth reading this paragraph just to see if you do.

Small cruelties are subtle. They include gestures and body language – like sighs, rolling the eyes, sneering lips, turning away etc.

They are a thousand little digs in the places where you are sensitive.

Let's say you are struggling at work. You talk to your partner about your problems, hoping for friendly feedback. Instead of that, you get indications that your issues and concerns are unimportant. Your pathetic handling of work situations is pointed out to you by the person you love.

What do you do? He's discounted your emotional needs.

It's hard to discuss the issue of discounting.

If your lover discounts the things that are important to you where do you turn? Instead of one problem you now have two. The work problem and the uncomfortable feeling that you are being 'got at' by your partner too.

And what if your partner is always well- behaved in front of your friends? They might not take your concerns seriously.

If your partner maintains a constant trickle of low-level, under-mining comments, and snide jokes at your expense in private – it might seem like a trivial situation.

As your self-worth drains away, you're more likely to blame yourself than your partner.

There are still good moments. Random acts of kindness on his side. But the sarcasm and nasty put-downs increase over time. It saps your self-esteem.

And as you become more and more nervous and afraid of whatever stupid mistake you think you might do next – knowing that whatever it is – he'll point it out to you as quickly as he can; you sink into traumatic bonding.

A MODERN-DAY TALE OF HANS MY HEDGEHOG

Here's an example of how Hans My Hedgehog might play out in a street near you:

Hans Valley-Smyth was a salesman.

Everyone said he was such a nice man. A bit arrogant, but also generous and caring. He met Carly, a nurse, on holiday in Morocco and it was love at first sight for Carly.

After three weeks they moved in together. She went to live with him in his smart flat overlooking the golf course. She left her friends behind and looked forward to a new life full of love and fun with Hans.

Not long after they started living together Hans showed another side of himself. He liked to have sex all night long. This made Carly very tired and after a few months, she got fired from work.

This seemed fine since Hans had often complained that her work got in the way of his life and she didn't earn enough money to make a difference to their standard of living.

In fact he seemed quite pleased. Now they could go on holiday without having to wait for the school holidays and be surrounded by brats abroad.

Carly set up a little online business working from home. But there were many late nights discussing and arguing over the things she did wrong and she was exhausted.

Her business got off to a slow start. She found it hard to get out of bed. Often, she'd find herself crying for no reason.

Then she found out that Hans had been telling everyone how lazy and inconsiderate she was. This hurt her deeply. She felt betrayed. Surely Hans knew how difficult she was finding the changes in her life?

When she tried to talk to him about it he just smiled.

When she cried with frustration he smiled even more.

When she told him she couldn't have so much sex, he accused her of behaving like an old woman.

His criticism of her made her feel like she was walking on eggshells. If she asked him not to talk to her in that way – he'd tell her he was joking.

She was very confused. Everyone thought he was a wonderful man and she loved him. He was wealthy enough to take her on lovely holidays and she didn't have to do a proper job.

In front of their friends he was always helpful, making coffee and jokes. All her friends thought she had the perfect relationship.

It was only when they were alone that he cut her with his sarcastic comments and made her feel small and useless.

Finally, Carly tried to talk to her family about what Hans was doing. But no one would listen.

She felt trapped and started having panic attacks.

In the end, she had to get anti-depressants from the doctor. She also became agoraphobic, frightened of everything outside in the world.

Whatever she did, Hans let her know how pathetic, deceitful and stupid he thought she was. Carly came to believe him.

THE END

QUICK WRITE

Find a quiet corner and curl up with your notebook.

Use this prompt to freewrite for 5 minutes.

What is sarcasm?

With the help of your IWW, explore this issue.

Why does it hurt?

Have you experienced it in your relationship?

How is it different from real humor?

CHAPTER 20
LITTLE RED RIDING HOOD

T his is the version recorded by Charles Perrault in 1697.

ONCE UPON A TIME THERE LIVED IN A CERTAIN VILLAGE A LITTLE *country girl, the prettiest creature who was ever seen.*

Her mother was excessively fond of her; and her grandmother doted on her still more. This good woman had a little red riding hood made for her child. It suited the girl so extremely well that everybody called her Little Red Riding Hood.

One day her mother, having made some cakes, said to her, "Go, my dear, and see how your grandmother is doing, for I hear she has been very ill. Take her a cake, and this little pot of butter."

Little Red Riding Hood set out immediately to go to her grandmother, who lived in another village.

As she was going through the wood, she met with a wolf, who had a very great mind to eat her up, but he dared not, because of some woodcutters working nearby in the forest.

He asked her where she was going.

The poor child, who did not know that it was dangerous to stay and talk to

a wolf, said to him, "I am going to see my grandmother and carry her a cake and
a little pot of butter from my mother."

"Does she live far off?" said the wolf

"Oh I say," answered Little Red Riding Hood; "it is beyond that mill you see
there, at the first house in the village."

"Well," said the wolf, "and I'll go and see her too. I'll go this way and go you
that, and we shall see who will be there first."

The wolf ran as fast as he could, taking the shortest path, and the little girl
took a roundabout way, entertaining herself by gathering nuts, running after
butterflies, and gathering bouquets of little flowers.

It was not long before the wolf arrived at the old woman's house. He
knocked at the door: tap, tap.

"Who's there?"

"Your grandchild, Little Red Riding Hood," replied the wolf, counterfeiting
her voice; "who has brought you a cake and a little pot of butter sent you by
mother."

The good grandmother, who was in bed because she was somewhat ill, cried
out, "Pull the bobbin, and the latch will go up."

The wolf pulled the bobbin, and the door opened, and then he immediately
fell upon the good woman and ate her up in a moment, for it been more than
three days since he had eaten.

He then shut the door and got into the grandmother's bed, expecting Little
Red Riding Hood, who came some time afterwards and knocked at the door:
tap, tap.

"Who's there?"

Little Red Riding Hood, hearing the big voice of the wolf, was at first
afraid; but believing her grandmother had a cold and was hoarse, answered, "It
is your grandchild Little Red Riding Hood, who has brought you a cake and a
little pot of butter mother sends you."

The wolf cried out to her, softening his voice as much as he could, "Pull the
bobbin, and the latch will go up."

Little Red Riding Hood pulled the bobbin, and the door opened.

The wolf, seeing her come in, said to her, hiding himself under the bedclothes,
"Put the cake and the little pot of butter upon the stool, and come get into bed
with me."

Little Red Riding Hood took off her clothes and got into bed. She was greatly amazed to see how her grandmother looked in her nightclothes, and said to her, "Grandmother, what big arms you have!"

"All the better to hug you with, my dear."

"Grandmother, what big legs you have!"

"All the better to run with, my child."

"Grandmother, what big ears you have!"

"All the better to hear with, my child."

"Grandmother, what big eyes you have!"

"All the better to see with, my child."

"Grandmother, what big teeth you have got!"

"All the better to eat you up with."

And, saying these words, this wicked wolf fell upon Little Red Riding Hood, and ate her all up.

PERRAULT'S MORAL TAKE ON THIS STORY...

"Children, especially attractive, well-bred young ladies, should never talk to strangers, for if they should do so, they may well provide dinner for a wolf. I say "wolf," but there are various kinds of wolves. There are also those who are charming, quiet, polite, unassuming, complacent, and sweet, who pursue young women at home and in the streets. And unfortunately, it is these gentle wolves who are the most dangerous ones of all."

IT'S LRRH'S FAULT

Little Red Riding Hood is to blame!

It's her fault that the wolf eats her. In this version of the story at least. Even though she did not know it was dangerous to talk to wolves.

And as Perrault points out at the end of his moral paragraph quoted above – ***these gentle wolves are the most dangerous of all.***

If you Google Little Red Riding Hood you'll probably be amazed to find the number of porn sites that come up.

Little Red, all alone, innocently trotting through the woods chasing butterflies appears to be a huge hit with a certain kind of pervert.

He enjoys defiling an innocent young woman.

This is what the wolf sets out to do as soon as he sees this girl. She's wearing red – the colour as we've seen – of sex and heat and lust and energy.

So she's giving out signals she doesn't understand.

And she's wearing a hood which might easily symbolise the clitoris, on top of her head.

So everything about her says: come and get me. Eat me up. I'm delicious.

However, all these signals are in the wolf's mind.

Actually, she's just grabbed her favourite coat and gone to visit her grandmother.

She isn't intending to become lunch for anyone.

LRRH GETS INTO BED WITH THE WOLF

Which must mean that she's definitely up for it.

The kind of wolf who plays out the LRRH scenario won't see his games as a problem for anyone.

This is because he finds it impossible to see the world from anyone else's point of view. He thinks Little Red is going to enjoy his company.

No really. He does.

He's a player, so you must be the same. Who isn't? He's having a good time. Why aren't you?

There are certain love words he knows.

When he says them in certain situations to certain women – hey presto – they let him come round and maybe even have lots of sex with him. They adore him. He's got admirers.

The love words are so useful he uses them on lots of different women. It works like a dream.

Only problem is, these women seem to think they've got some kind of a hold on him. Especially if he's married them or moved into their house or whatever.

They nag him if he's late, cry when they see him flirting with another woman. It's all very annoying for him.

Look at it from his point of view. He likes to be admired and loved.

He likes to have lots of sex and/or attention from loads of different women.

He was put on this earth to enjoy the female body. So why are they always trying to spoil it for him? It's his life after all.

THIS IS THE SEXIEST WOLF

He might not be that good-looking but he's got sexual charisma oozing out of him like engine oil from a biker's beard.

And whatever he's got, he knows how to use it. He might be all dressed up in nice lady's clothes (yes, the wolf in LRRH is sometimes called the 'transvestite wolf') but he's all man and he'll go all night like a wild animal if you let him.

Then he'll go off and find some other woman to do his thing with.

This is a really hard story to live in. He's bad for you. You know this because it's obvious.

He flirts so much it's embarrassing and it hurts.

But for some reason, you end up angrier with the other women in his life than with him.

Why? Stockholm syndrome again.

You love him – that's real.

But he's twisted your mind by telling you he loves you. However, he's confused poor thing. After all, that other woman is such a distraction. She's nice. He likes her a lot. He loves you too – but you're different from her.

Oh dear. He likes you both so much. He doesn't know what to do. He just can't help himself. And so on and so on.

He's probably told the other woman or women in his life all sorts of terrible things about you. And he still wants you. So you might even end up in a bad scene with her rather than taking it out on him.

Of course, he'll love this. If you two ever fight over him, he'll be watching and enjoying every moment if he can.

You'll see his big teeth, his hairy hands and his wolfish grin but somehow, you just can't get him out of your bed.

Until it's too late. He's eaten up your soul.

How did he do this?

By Eating Granny...

The grandmother in Perrault's version ends up being eaten alive.

She isn't rescued by any hunters either.

What might this symbolise? Well, the kindly grandmother motif appears as an archetype in myths and legends around the world.

Who might she represent psychologically?

My personal interpretation on this is that granny is the **Inner Wise Woman** who belongs to Little Red.

Remember, the **IWW** is your intuition. Your nurturing, wise and loving self. Once the wolf has control of this – or has separated you from this side of yourself – he has control over you.

But don't worry. You can wake her up. Pick up a pen and a notebook and write your way back to her. She's always there. The wolf can never destroy her.

A Modern Version of Little Red Riding Hood

Once upon a time a woman called Scarlet went to visit her grandmother in the old people's home.

On the way there she ran into an old friend from school called Tim. Tim asked her out for a drink. He had lovely eyes and kept staring at her in a way that made her shiver with excitement.

'Come for a drink with me?' he said.

'But I've got to visit my gran.'

'Come on. Have a little fun in your life.'

She checked her watch. Grandmother would be asleep so Scarlet figured she had time for a quick one.

They went to a lovely pub by a bubbling river.

Tim bought her a fabulous lunch and told Scarlet all about his great job in a furniture warehouse and the awful woman he was married to.

'It was a mistake to get married,' he said, his face dropping. 'She forced me into it.'

'Oh, that's terrible,' Scarlet said, wondering how any man could be forced into marriage nowadays, but he was so sweet and so believable.

'I don't know what to do,' he said, 'I feel like I'm in hell. Can you help me crawl out of it?'

He reached out and stroked her cheek.

She felt so sorry for him.

And she was thinking he'd be fun in bed.

Later that afternoon after a bottle of Pinot Grigio, she found out. He was fun in bed. And enthusiastic and passionate. Afterwards, he told her he felt happy for the first time in years. And it was all down to her.

Scarlet glowed with satisfaction.

Now Scarlet herself had just come out of a bad relationship so she understood what Tim was going through. They started to meet secretly once a week, and spent a lot of time discussing how unhappy Tim was. Afterwards, they'd both make him happy in bed.

'I'm going to leave that bitch I'm married to,' Tim said.

Scarlet was overjoyed.

'Thank God. You deserve to be happy Tim.'

'She's mental though,' Tim said. 'I'm worried she might do something stupid if I leave.'

The next day Scarlet went round to Tim's house. They were in bed together when his wife, Emerald, came home early. She was so angry with Scarlet she dragged her out of bed and pulled her hair and threw her on the floor, weeping and shouting.

She really is mad, Scarlet thought. Poor Tim.

Soon afterwards Emerald divorced Tim and started a new life as a wildlife ranger in Scotland. Good riddance!

Scarlet moved in with Tim but soon after that she discovered Tim was seeing her sister, Ruby.

Scarlet thought about suicide.

Finally, she went to visit her grandmother. But nothing gave her any pleasure any more. Not even the old lady with her funny hat.

'Your sister tells me you've gone crazy,' grandmother said. 'She says your boyfriend told her you forced him to have a relationship with him while he was happily married...'

'What?' Scarlet said. 'You must have got it wrong granny.'

'Oh no, we've had long chats about how happy Tim makes her.'

Scarlet felt her heart grow cold. 'Go on.'

'Well, your sister really likes him. She even brought him here for a visit. He's quite attractive and so attentive. He told me that being with you is like a living hell.'

Scarlet stumbled out into the cold winter afternoon; feeling like her brain was in a blender.

The End.

QUICK WRITE

In your notebook write out the question:

What is honesty?

And just write anything that comes out.

Give it 5 minutes.

This might seem too simple a question to write about at first. But it isn't.

Think about the times you've lied to protect your own feelings or someone else's.

There are big lies and little ones.

What kind of honesty matters?

Is faithfulness important to you in a relationship?

Have you ever been unfaithful?

Have you fallen in love with a man already in a relationship?

Do you think he was faithful to you?

Did you want him to be? Why?

Did you care about how his partner would feel if she found out?

What kind of a man cheats on his wife/girlfriend/lover?

If your wolf cheated on you - who did you blame most – him or the other woman?

Are women unkind to each other when it comes to the love of a desirable man?

CHAPTER 21
THE LITTLE MERMAID

"Of all Anderson's characters, it is probably the Little Mermaid who is
the real virtuoso in the art of silent suffering."
Maria Tatar

ONCE, A LITTLE MERMAID LIVED AT THE BOTTOM OF A DEEP OCEAN.
*Her loving family included her father, Triton, King of the Sea, six older sisters
and her grandmother.*

*At the age of fifteen she was allowed to swim to the surface and see the
world above.*

*While she was there a storm blew up and the Little Mermaid saved the life
of a drowning man by sculling him to shore. She fell in love with him instantly
and discovered he was a prince. But she was a mermaid and he was a human
with an eternal soul so she had to leave him.*

Lovesick and forlorn she asked the sea witch for help.

*The witch agreed to give the Little Mermaid legs in exchange for the girl's
tongue.*

*With legs, every step the Little Mermaid took was like walking on swords
and her feet bled as if she'd walked on glass.*

If the Little Mermaid could marry the prince then she would get an immortal soul. But if she failed, she would die and become nothing more than sea foam.

At first, the prince is attracted to the beauty of the Little Mermaid. He loves to see her dance and she is graceful – even though every step is agony for her and makes her feet bleed.

However, the prince's father tells him to marry the daughter of a neighbouring king.

At first the prince tells the Little Mermaid that he won't marry the other woman because he's in love with the woman who saved his life and the Little Mermaid reminds him of her.

Because she can't speak, the Little Mermaid can't tell him that she was the one who saved him and left him at the temple.

For a brief moment the Little Mermaid seems to have won his heart. But when the prince discovers that the other woman lives at the temple – he believes her to be the one that saved him and so he marries her instead.

On their wedding day the Little Mermaid is cursed – and she knows that she will die the next morning.

The Little Mermaid feels her heart break at this time and she thinks of all she has given up and all her suffering.

In the night her sisters come up from the sea with a magic knife. If the Little Mermaid kills the prince and rubs his blood on her feet, she will get back her tail and be able to return home to the sea. She goes to his bedside but cannot bring herself to kill the man she loves.

The next morning the Little Mermaid jumps into the sea and dissolves into cold sea foam.

The End

THE POWER OF THE STORY...

There is a statue of the Little Mermaid in Copenhagen harbour.

About 75% of tourists who visit the city go to see her. It's like a pilgrimage.

What are they looking for?

Why is she such a powerful symbol of lost love? Or indeed, of feminine rejection and humiliation?

The statue is lovely – but surprisingly small. She's simply a naked woman on a rock. She stares wistfully out to sea towards her real home. She's got legs but if you look closely, her feet are similar to fishtails.

The deep meaning of this statue is so strong that she's been a victim of regular vandalism. Her head was sawn off a couple of times, red paint thrown over her, a bra painted over her breasts and famously a dildo was once strapped to her head.

If you ever doubted the power of ancient stories and the characters within them, it's worth looking carefully at the Little Mermaid and the sacrifices she made for love.

Do you know what it feels like to give up your voice?

Does your lover tell you what to say or what not to say in every situation?

Have you forgotten what your opinions are?

Does he sob if you offend him?

If so, you might have cast your own ideas, feelings and problems aside for a wolf with so many of his own that there isn't any room for yours.

There's no room for your voice either - or your feelings. Actually, there's no room for you in the relationship.

In the end, you probably feel as if you're invisible.

Like a bubble of foam after a wave has crashed on the beach.

Over time, the wolf that casts you in The Little Mermaid role will keep you hanging on because he's so good at pretending he's sensitive and caring.

He's in touch with his feminine side.

This is symbolised by the watery environment of this story. Water is a potent representation of the emotions. This wolf is wise to this – and he sails the high seas looking for caring, loving women he can fool into believing he's a kindly beta male.

His Emotions are More Equal that Yours...

This is the kind of wolf who'll persuade you that he thinks men and women are equal.

Only problem is that to him, this means only one thing. **His emotions are much more equal than yours.**

He might cry buckets and need comforting from you. But if you're crying – you cry alone.

He's playing the part of the sensitive, poetic prince who can give you an immortal soul. But only if you love him enough. Of course, you never can.

Even if he doesn't love another woman, he probably loves himself more than you. Soon it because clear that you're so far out of your comfort zone there's no way back. Not only have you lost direction like Karen in the Red Shoes, you've lost your natural habitat.

Mermaids should live in the sea.

Walking on land with magical legs, according to this story, will always feel like walking on knives.

You might have seen the Disney version in which Ariel marries Prince Eric after various adventures and they all live happily ever after.

Wrong story.

The original tale is much darker and sadder.

The Little Mermaid sacrifices her soul for love. In other words, she gives up her true Self in her quest to win the Prince – who rejects her anyway.

Let's have a closer look at the story:

If you weren't timid before...

A relationship with this wolf will turn you into a mouse.

He's so sure of how right he is about everything that you can't help agreeing with him.

Besides, arguing with him is so exhausting and you always, always end up feeling guilty about hurting such a great guy.

After all he really is great - isn't he? He's told you so many times about his achievements. He'll explain how many people love him, how popular he is. You're dazzled by his caring personality. And at the same time so grateful he has chosen to love you.

When your friends meet him they think he's a New Man. Even if his love only lasts as long as it takes for him to find another woman to impress all over again.

The Little Mermaid gives up her natural element – water. To live on land with legs is excruciatingly painful – just walking on solid ground makes her feet bleed. However, the prince likes to see her dance and so she does it for him.

Can't he spot the pain in her eyes? Almost certainly not.

And if he does, perhaps he doesn't care. Or even worse, maybe he's secretly enjoying it.

The Little Mermaid loses her power in three crucial areas.

- She leaves her world, the element of water in order to live on land.
- She swaps her tail for human legs and a lifetime of pain.
- And thirdly, she loses her voice. It's a huge sacrifice and it gets her nowhere.

FEET AND DANCING – REPETITION OF A THEME.

There are some themes we all understand on an unconscious level. The level at which the symbolism of fairy tales really operate.

Bringing to light these symbols and themes helps us to understand how we've lost our power. Doing this also gives us clues as to how we can reclaim it over time.

The Little Mermaid is another story with an emphasis on feet and dancing.

When it came to the Red Shoes, by enchanting her feet – the wolf takes away Karen's direction in life forcing her to dance aimlessly until she dies.

In the Little Mermaid, the poor girl dances willingly for the prince because it pleases him.

She does this despite the fact that it's agony for her.

Dancing, even nowadays has links with joy, loss of inhibitions, and sexuality.

Just turn on the TV and watch the latest music videos.

What do you see?

In most cases, half-naked nymphs gyrate hypnotically. It's more like the kind of soft porn men enjoy when they're alone than something shared and joyful for all.

Obviously, The Red Shoes and The Little Mermaid stories are hinting at something more than a few whirls across the dance floor.

What makes a woman bleed apart from her natural cycle? Childbirth. Losing her virginity. Menstruation. Blood and women's fertility and sexuality are inextricably linked.

If you replace the word 'sex' with 'dancing' you might have a clue as to the deeper meaning in these tales.

One of the key issues in emotional abuse of women is sexual coercion.

Maybe your wolf wants sex or wanted it more than you do – but you can't refuse him.

Maybe he knows what satisfies you but withholds it as a method of control. Yes, men use this trick too and it's fairly common among wolves. One month he wears you out with his needs and the next he turns his back on you as soon as you get naked.

Neither option is going to make you feel good about yourself and it's not designed to.

WHAT IS IT LIKE TO HAVE NO VOICE?

Not only has the Little Mermaid lost direction in her life by leaving her natural element, she's also lost her voice.

It's difficult enough to lose your voice when it happens through illness. You can't join in conversations or call for help. At least these days most of us can write so we've got a method of communication open to us.

But this is a fairy tale so the 'voice' is a symbol of something far deeper.

Going back to folklore; mermaids were famous for their lovely singing.

Some stories say they sang so beautifully it would drive men wild. Ships would crash on rocks trying to get to the singers. Men would throw themselves in the sea and drown trying to catch a hold of the singer. In paintings, stories and songs - mermaids and water nymphs were depicted as beautiful, nubile young women, combing their long hair, singing away and cavorting in the waves like dolphins.

Sounds like enough to drive any man crazy.

If we remember that the underlying psychology of emotionally abusive wolves is their misogyny – then the Little Mermaid character is a really big problem for him. She's got the power – symbolically speaking – to destroy him. One of her greatest assets is her voice – her soul, her inner beauty. It has a beguiling, haunting quality and in the mind of a wolf – it must be stopped.

We each have two voices.

Firstly, there's the kind you make sounds with through your vocal chords.

Secondly, there's the inner voice. Your second voice is more than just your inner monologue.

Your inner voice is your spontaneous unique take on things. It's about your attitudes, opinions, sense of humour. Your likes and dislikes. The way you express all your emotions. Your heart and soul – that's your inner voice.

Because we all know that relationships involve compromise it's easy to see how a woman falling into the 'Little Mermaid' trap gets into this role.

Slowly.

Very slowly. If this is your story, then you've got less and less to say about anything as time goes by. This is partly because he's got all the answers.

If you disagree with him on the smallest point you get shouted down.

You get shouted down more often as the relationship goes on until your inner voice is so quiet you can hardly hear it. Besides, he is so wounded anyway. And your opinions, attitudes, approach to life and ideas etc. add to his wounding.

So you stop trying to trying to express them. He's so sensitive. You don't want to hurt him.

So instead, you suffer.

A sure sign that this is your story is if you've grown more timid over your time with him especially when he's around.

Maybe, every once in a while in a group of friends you're the same person you used to be. Happy, funny, chatty and with lots of views about stuff.

But when you're with him it's a different story.

Shy and tongue-tied, you don't know what to think unless he tells you. You're terrified of hurting his feelings. You're walking on knives. You've lost your Self in his world, his story.

WATER IS A SYMBOL AS BIG AS THE OCEAN.

The Little Mermaid lives in an exciting aquatic world. She moves through it with ease and pleasure. Going back a few million years or so we were all water creatures. Our bodies are still largely made up of water and we die quicker without water than without food.

So water is important from a biological point of view.

Symbolically water holds a whole host of meanings.

Often used as a motif for the unconscious mind because almost everything is hidden below the surface, it's also associated with the imagination.

In the Tarot, the suit of cups (the cups are for holding or spilling water according the card's meaning) morphed into hearts in the modern-day pack of playing cards for good reason.

Water stood for the emotions.

Most particularly – the emotion of love.

A woman who is good at love, someone who is imaginative, and a deep thinker is a powerful being. Her power is a great challenge for the sensitive wolf who loves to compete and come out on top.

He's only pretending to have a heart.

You've got a real one.

Apart from anything else, it's a jealousy thing.

There's nothing wrong with your element. Nothing wrong with being sensitive and loving. Water is deep and full of strange and wonderful creatures, and if you feel drawn to return to it – then you must.

WHY DOES THE PRINCE REJECT HER IN THE END?

Right through this story, the prince is in control.

In the end, the Little Mermaid dies.

Once again we'll approach this as a symbol. A part of you dies or is lost because of the relationship. Don't worry. This isn't a permanent state.

It can leave you heartbroken and suffering but recovery is possible and we'll see how when you put everything together using the DIOL method.

However, the saddest thing about this story is that the prince rejects the Little Mermaid because she's lost the very things that made her so attractive and special.

The things she gave up to be with him. Ironic isn't it? Not really. When the prince is using his power to gain control over the mermaid – she's a challenge and he finds her exciting.

But once she's compliant and submissive he gets bored. He has to move on to the next challenge, the next woman, the next relationship.

What attracted him to the Little Mermaid at the beginning was the fact that she was free.

She could swim, sing, feel things deeply.

She had a rich inner life symbolised by her element, water.

By the time she's left all that behind to fit into his world he doesn't want her any more.

If you're a sensitive woman and you feel as if you've given up your voice, both inner and outer, perhaps this is your story.

A MODERN VERSION OF THE LITTLE MERMAID:

Not long ago or very far away, a woman called Martha was out running in the park.

She loved running, swimming and cycling – in fact she was a triathlete in her spare time.

She'd won a few races and took her training seriously. She lived in a shared house with a gaggle of friends from university and she had a nice job in a cosy office.

Well, one day it was raining hard and her route took her down by the river. She was shocked to see a man fall off a bridge into the water.

Martha dived in and dragged the stranger to the shore. When he woke up it was love at first sight.

His name was Ralph, and he ran a farm two hundred miles away from where Martha lived. But she was so in love that within three months, she'd moved in with him.

He was very proud of his collection of prize cattle and was keen for Martha to join him in business.

She learned all she could about farming cattle. There was no time for her to train anymore but she didn't mind.

Sure, she missed her friends and all the locals in the nearest village were pretty unfriendly but she tried as hard as she could to fit in.

For a couple of years she worked harder than she'd ever worked in her life. She was up before dawn and seldom went to bed before midnight.

Ralph became more and more distant unless he wanted sex, in which case he'd often keep her up all night.

She knew he needed to spend his time in his office doing paperwork and having meetings with other farmers in town.

One day, Martha found out he'd been seeing someone else, a woman called Ellen.

Ellen was one of Martha's friends – another athlete who competed in horse trials all over the country.

Ellen was at the peak of fitness and also ran her own gym.

Martha on the other hand, was no longer strong and fit – not like she used to be.

Her back had suffered with all the hauling about on the farm and she'd broken her arm in a milking accident. She was very lonely.

For days at a time she spoke to no one and she felt isolated, unloved and shy.

Then, Ralph told her he wanted to live with Ellen instead.

Martha felt her heart breaking.

In the end, Martha was trampled by cattle as she ran across a field crying her eyes out as she thought of everything she'd given up for Ralph.

The End.

QUICK WRITE

Sit with your notebook a while and imagine your IWW sitting with you. When you feel her warm, loving and wise presence, write this question at the top of the page:

Have I given up my voice for love?

Write for about five minutes.

Read back what you've written afterwards.

If you've got more to say then write it.

You can set it out as a letter.

Don't send it. Just write it.

There. That's your own voice on the page, coming to the surface again.

Welcome back.

CHAPTER 22
THE ROBBER BRIDEGROOM...

J acob and Wilhelm Grimm, first published 1812.

A MILLER WISHED TO MARRY HIS DAUGHTER OFF, AND SO WHEN A RICH
suitor appeared, he betrothed her to him.

One day the suitor complained that the daughter never visited him, told her
that he lived in the forest, and overrode her reluctance by telling her he would
leave a trail of ashes so she could find his home.

She filled her pockets with peas and lentils and marked the trail with them
as she followed the ashes.

They led her to a dark and silent house.

A bird in a cage called out to warn her that she entered a murderer's house.

An old woman in a cellar kitchen told her that the people there would kill
and eat her unless the old woman protected her and hid her behind a barrel.

A band of robbers arrived with a young woman, and they killed her and
prepared to eat her.

When one chopped off a finger to get at the golden ring on it, the finger and
ring flew through the air and landed in the bodice of the hiding woman.

The old woman discouraged them from searching, because the neither finger nor the ring were likely to run away: they'd find it in the morning.

The old woman drugged the robbers' wine.

As soon as they fell asleep, the two living women fled. Wind had blown the ashes away, but the peas and lentils had sprung up into seedlings: the two followed the path of plants and reached the young woman's home.

When the wedding day arrived and the guests were telling stories, the young woman said that she would tell a dream she had had, and told of her visit to the robbers' den, her bridegroom punctuating it with "My darling, you only dreamed this," until she produced the finger of the dead girl and showed it to the company.

The robber bridegroom and his entire band were put to death.

The End

THE ROBBER BRIDEGROOM LIVES DEEP IN THE FOREST...

The forest of his own imagination. Here, he is king. He lives outside the accepted rules of behaviour. Not only is he a thief, which is how he makes his money, but he's also a cannibal.

We'll look at these two aspects of the Robber Bridegroom later, but for now, let's have a journey through the deep, dark forest of the mind.

Forests often appear as places full of magic and danger in fairy tales.

Sometimes they offer refuge, but usually bad things happen there. Perhaps it's because it's easy to get lost in them.

They used to be full of wild animals. Predators. The kind of creatures that might kill and eat a person straying off the path.

Transformation is likely to happen in forests. Nothing is quite what it seems. For the unwary traveller, especially the young bride-to-be in this story, one step into the forest might be a step too far.

Dreaming you are lost in a forest might mean you're feeling overwhelmed.

And forests can also symbolise the darkest recesses of the unconscious mind, which is also the home of desire, transformation, dreams, growth, danger and love.

In this story, the young bride has a hunch that all is not well.

She leaves a trail of lentils to guide her back home. Just in case.

For many women entering relationships with emotionally abusive men, there is a subconscious awareness that he might not be everything he appears to be.

They make sure they know their way back home.

Even if they forget what they know for a time.

Remember, the seeds they threw have grown along the path to show you the way back.

POWERFUL WOLVES ARE ADDICTED TO POWER

So often it's easy to see why women are attracted to a certain kind of wolf.

He might not be that sexy or good-looking. But if he's successful and powerful in his own way, he'll have a kind of charisma. A certain swagger. An air of potency.

For thousands of years women looked for these attributes in a mate.

A capable, virile man would provide for her and the healthy children he gave her. It's easy to mock this kind of situation, but that doesn't mean it's easy to turn it down if love comes into the equation.

Loving attention from a man like this is hard to resist.

The problems begin when a man like this turns out to be a wolf addicted to power.

He'll expect to have this powerful feeling in every avenue of his life. That includes his relationships.

If it means cutting a woman into small pieces with his verbal and psychological abuse, then that's what he'll do.

It won't matter to him.

The game is all about winning, about getting what he wants.

He won't see you as a person, but as part of his collection.

In his eyes, he'll own you.

THERE'S MORE THAN ONE WAY TO SKIN A CAT

In the 1980s, in a cave in Cheddar Gorge, Somerset, the remains of human bones about 14,700 years old were found.

Marks on these bones show they were butchered and the marrow removed.

Forensic archaeologists believe this is evidence of ritual killing and cannibalism.

The taboo of eating our own species is as strong as ever. Perhaps it was more of a religious practise than a taste for flesh, but it's been a dark part human history in almost all cultures.

However, there's more than one way to skin a cat or indeed, to devour another person.

To do this, you break them down emotionally, mentally, and psychologically piece by piece.

A man once told me that the ultimate form of love was symbolised by a snake slowly devouring itself starting with its tail. Love? I don't think so. Sounds more like suffocation.

The Robber Bridegroom story also makes me think about vampires. Various legends about vampires – those who feed on the blood of others – have been knocking around Europe and many other countries for thousands of years.

Take away the folklore and what have you got?

Psychic vampires.

People who drain you. You know the type. If you spend too much time with them, you feel totally exhausted.

They make you feel a little crazy. But what if you fall in love with one? Every day they get to drain a little bit more of your energy, your enthusiasm, your love of life.

In the story it doesn't say how long the Robber Bridegroom tormented his victims before he killed them.

Perhaps he chopped them to bits over a period of time. There's something about his dark house hidden in the dark woods which suggests this might have been the case.

It's true that all emotionally abusive men are psychic vampires in one way or another.

And in the story of the Robber Bridegroom (RB), the woman (who is never named) is taking part in an arranged marriage rather than a love match. The RB is rich, so we are told, and the woman's father tells her to marry him.

However, if this was a love match, the bride-to-be might still follow her instinct and leave a trail of lentils.

People can demand so much of others that in effect, they devour them.

They eat your time, your confidence and your ability to think for yourself.

An emotionally abusive wolf of the RB type will be odd right from the start. He's fussy and precise. He sees himself as a maverick.

If you get to know about his past, you'll find at least one 'severed ring finger'. This might be a previous wife (he'll tell you it was all her fault the marriage ended), or a broken, damaged ex- girlfriend who tries to tell you what he's really like.

Too late, you realise she was telling the truth. Her warning is useful though.

Always be alert for the truth of his past relationships.

Leaving this kind of wolf can be very dangerous.

He's the kind who might get violent.

A MODERN-DAY TALE OF THE ROBBER BRIDEGROOM

Once upon a time in a street near you, a young woman called Rose met a rich man called Keith at a barbecue.

They laughed and laughed the whole afternoon and got quite drunk together.

Rose had been recently made redundant from her job as a classroom assistant and was struggling to pay the bills. Keith had piercing eyes and stood very close to Rose. He made her forget her troubles.

Afterwards, Keith drove Rose home and kissed her passionately at the door.

The next day, Rose rang her father, a fat, greedy man who was frightened that Rose might start asking him for money.

'Oh my god,' Rose said, 'I've met this new guy and he's got an Aston Martin.'

'That's a very expensive car,' Rose's dad said. 'You better hang on to that one.'

Rose frowned. 'He's a bit weird,' she said.

She couldn't put her finger on it, but something about Keith made her feel uncomfortable.

'What's the matter girl? Don't look a gift horse in the mouth.'

'You're right, dad. I'm just scared of falling in love.'

Three months later, after a lot of wining and dining in wonderful restaurants and a couple of weekends away in lovely country hotels, Keith asked Rose to marry him.

She agreed and moved in to his chocolate box cottage in the forest, far from all her family.

'This is how we do things around here,' Keith said. 'The beds are changed every Tuesday, the house cleaned every day and I only eat home-cooked food. You're not doing anything at the moment so you're in charge of all that.'

After a few months, Rose became increasingly unhappy.

She never seemed to do anything right. Her housework was not up to the correct standard. Keith was cross with her most of the time.

Sometimes, she thought he was going to hit her. Once, he pushed her so hard during an argument that he bruised her ribs.

'You made me do that,' Keith said. 'You're so difficult.'

One night, Rose met Keith's ex-wife, Jo, at a friend's house.

Rose was hardly allowed out without Keith and was looking forward to a nice evening. Instead, she got a bit weepy but she didn't know why.

Jo told her that being married to Keith was like being locked up in prison. He terrorised her and made her have sex with other men in front of her.

'You're just jealous,' Rose said and left the friend's house.

'Never go round there again,' Keith told Rose when she got home that night. 'You don't need any friends. You've got me.'

Five months later, Rose started having sex with other men in front of Keith. It made her feel sick – it just wasn't her thing.

The luxury lifestyle was all Keith's. She felt like a housemaid and an accessory to him. S

he hated her life and didn't know how she got into this mess.

The End

QUICK WRITE

Take your notebook and pen out into the countryside or a nearby park.

Find a tree and sit underneath it.

Use this question as a prompt and write for five minutes only:

What does it feel like to be lost?

Let your **IWW's** love flow down your arm, through your pen and onto the page.

Let her show you how you really feel.

Read back what you've written.

Can you see any clues as to how you might find yourself again?

Where does your trail of lentils lead?

Where in your body does that 'lost' feeling live?

Have you done things for your wolf you were ashamed of?

CHAPTER 23
BLUEBEARD

*T*his is Perrault's version, published 1697.

THERE WAS ONCE A MAN WHO HAD FINE HOUSES, A DEAL OF SILVER AND gold plate, embroidered furniture, and coaches gilded all over with gold.

But this man was so unlucky as to have a blue beard, which made him so ugly that all the women ran away from him.

One of his neighbours, a lady of quality, had two daughters who were perfect beauties.

He desired of her one of them in marriage, leaving to her choice which of the two she would bestow on him. Neither of them would have him, and they sent him backwards and forwards from one to the other, not being able to bear the thoughts of marrying a man who had a blue beard.

Adding to their disgust and aversion was the fact that he already had been married to several wives, and nobody knew what had become of them.

Bluebeard, to engage their affection, took them, with their mother and three or four ladies of their acquaintance, with other young people of the neighbourhood, to one of his country houses, where they stayed a whole week.

The time was filled with parties, hunting, fishing, dancing, mirth, and feasting.

Nobody went to bed, but all passed the night in rallying and joking with each other.

In short, everything succeeded so well that the youngest daughter began to think that the man's beard was not so very blue after all, and that he was a mighty civil gentleman.

As soon as they returned home, the marriage was concluded.

About a month afterwards, Bluebeard told his wife that he was obliged to take a country journey for six weeks at least.

"Here," said he, "are the keys to the two great wardrobes, wherein I have my best furniture. These are to my silver and gold plate, which is not everyday in use. These open my strongboxes, which hold my money, both gold and silver; these my caskets of jewels.

And this is the master key to all my apartments.

But as for this little one here, it is the key to the closet at the end of the great hall on the ground floor.

Open them all; go into each and every one of them, except that little closet, which I forbid you, and forbid it in such a manner that, if you happen to open it, you may expect my just anger and resentment."

She promised to observe, very exactly, whatever he had ordered.

Then he, after having embraced her, got into his coach and proceeded on his journey.

Her neighbours and good friends did not wait to be sent for by the newly married lady.

They were impatient to see all the rich furniture of her house, and had not dared to come while her husband was there, because of his blue beard, which frightened them.

They ran through all the rooms, closets, and wardrobes, which were all so fine and rich that they seemed to surpass one another.

After that, they went up into the two great rooms, which contained the best and richest furniture.

They could not sufficiently admire the number and beauty of the tapestry, beds, couches, cabinets, stands, tables, and looking glasses, in which you might see yourself from head to foot; some of them were framed with glass, others with silver, plain and gilded, the finest and most magnificent that they had ever seen.

They ceased not to extol and envy the happiness of their friend, who in the meantime in no way diverted herself in looking upon all these rich things, because of the impatience she had to go and open the closet on the ground floor.

She was so much pressed by her curiosity that, without considering that it was very uncivil for her to leave her company, she went down a little back staircase, and with such excessive haste that she nearly fell and broke her neck.

Having come to the closet door, she made a stop for some time thinking about her husband's orders, and considering what unhappiness might attend her if she was disobedient; but the temptation was so strong that she could not overcome it.

She then took the little key, and opened it, trembling. At first she could not see anything plainly, because the windows were shut.

After some moments she began to perceive that the floor was all covered over with clotted blood, on which lay the bodies of several dead women, ranged against the walls.

(These were all the wives whom Bluebeard had married and murdered, one after another.)

She thought she should have died for fear, and the key, which she, pulled out of the lock, fell out of her hand.

After having somewhat recovered her surprise, she picked up the key, locked the door, and went upstairs into her chamber to recover; but she could not, so much was she frightened.

Having observed that the key to the closet was stained with blood, she tried two or three times to wipe it off; but the blood would not come out; in vain did she wash it, and even rub it with soap and sand.

The blood still remained, for the key was magical and she could never make it quite clean; when

the blood was gone off from one side, it came again on the other.

Bluebeard returned from his journey the same evening, saying that he had received letters upon the road, informing him that the affair he went about had concluded to his advantage.

His wife did all she could to convince him that she was extremely happy about his speedy return. The next morning he asked her for the keys, which she gave him, but with such a trembling hand that he easily guessed what had happened.

"What!" said he, "is not the key of my closet among the rest?"

"I must," said she, "have left it upstairs upon the table."

"Fail not," said Bluebeard, "to bring it to me at once."

After several goings backwards and forwards, she was forced to bring him the key. Bluebeard, having very attentively considered it, said to his wife, "Why is there blood on the key?"

"I do not know," cried the poor woman, paler than death.

"You do not know!" replied Bluebeard. "I very well know. You went into the closet, did you not? Very well, madam; you shall go back, and take your place among the ladies you saw there."

Upon this she threw herself at her husband's feet, and begged his pardon with all the signs of a true repentance, vowing that she would never more be disobedient.

She would have melted a rock, so beautiful and sorrowful was she; but Bluebeard had a heart harder than any rock!

"You must die, madam," said he, "at once."

"Since I must die," answered she (looking upon him with her eyes all bathed in tears), "give me some little time to say my prayers."

"I give you," replied Bluebeard, "half a quarter of an hour, but not one moment more."

When she was alone she called out to her sister, and said to her, "Sister Anne" (for that was her name), "go up, I beg you, to the top of the tower, and look if my brothers are not coming. They promised me that they would come today, and if you see them, give them a sign to make haste."

Her sister Anne went up to the top of the tower, and the poor afflicted wife cried out from time to time, "Anne, sister Anne, do you see anyone coming?"

And sister Anne said, "I see nothing but a cloud of dust in the sun, and the green grass."

In the meanwhile Bluebeard, holding a great sabre in his hand, cried out as loud as he could bawl to his wife, "Come down instantly, or I shall come up to you."

"One moment longer, if you please," said his wife; and then she cried out very softly, "Anne, sister Anne, do you see anybody coming?"

And sister Anne answered, "I see nothing but a cloud of dust in the sun, and the green grass."

"Come down quickly," cried Bluebeard, "or I will come up to you."

"I am coming," answered his wife; and then she cried, "Anne, sister Anne, do you not see anyone coming?"

"I see," replied sister Anne, "a great cloud of dust approaching us."

"Are they my brothers?"

"Alas, no my dear sister, I see a flock of sheep." "Will you not come down?" cried Bluebeard.

"One moment longer," said his wife, and then she cried out, "Anne, sister Anne, do you see nobody coming?"

"I see," said she, "two horsemen, but they are still a great way off."

"God be praised," replied the poor wife joyfully. "They are my brothers. I will make them a sign, as well as I can for them to make haste."

Then Bluebeard bawled out so loud that he made the whole house tremble.

The distressed wife came down, and threw herself at his feet, all in tears, with her hair about her shoulders.

"This means nothing," said Bluebeard. "You must die!"

Then, taking hold of her hair with one hand, and lifting up the sword with the other, he prepared to strike off her head. The poor lady, turning about to him, and looking at him with dying eyes, desired him to afford her one little moment to recollect herself.

"No, no," said he, "commend yourself to God," and was just ready to strike.

At this very instant there was such a loud knocking at the gate that Bluebeard made a sudden stop.

The gate was opened, and two horsemen entered.

Drawing their swords, they ran directly to Bluebeard.

He knew them to be his wife's brothers, one a dragoon, the other a musketeer; so that he ran away immediately to save himself; but the two brothers pursued and overtook him before he could get to the steps of the porch.

Then they ran their swords through his body and left him dead.

The poor wife was almost as dead as her husband, and had not strength enough to rise and welcome her brothers.

Bluebeard had no heirs, and so his wife became mistress of all his estate.

She made use of one part of it to marry her sister Anne to a young gentleman who had loved her a long while; another part to buy captains' commissions for her brothers, and the rest to marry herself to a very worthy gentleman, who made her forget the ill time she had passed with Bluebeard.

The End

CHARLES PERRAULT'S MORALS OF BLUEBEARD

"*Moral:* *Curiosity, in spite of its appeal, often leads to deep regret. To the displeasure of many a maiden, its enjoyment is short lived. Once satisfied, it ceases to exist, and always costs dearly.*

Another moral: *Apply logic to this grim story, and you will ascertain that it took place many years ago. No husband of our age would be so terrible as to demand the impossible of his wife, nor would he be such a jealous malcontent. For, whatever the colour of her husband's beard, the wife of today will let him know who the master is.*"

LET'S UNPICK THESE 'MORALS' ONE AT A TIME.

MORAL ONE: WOMEN SHOULD NOT BE CURIOUS...

It might get them killed.

Thank you Charles Perrault for that little gem of insight.

However, he was writing in the seventeenth century and things are very different now. Aren't they?

Actually, even today some men really don't like women who try to work things out with their brain.

A curious man is rewarded of course. He's a scientist or an interested observer of life – a philosopher. Up until a few years ago it was fashionable for mothers to warn their daughters not to appear too intelligent in mixed company because: it puts men off.

It doesn't put all men off. Some of them like an interesting conversation and a woman who likes to work things out with her brain.

However, if Bluebeard is your story, thinking, asking questions and general curiosity can get you into more trouble than its worth.

But you won't know this until it's too late, until you're so embedded in the relationship – perhaps married with children.

MORAL TWO: MEN NOWADAYS WOULD NEVER BEHAVE like that...

The reason for that - according to Perrault is that the women of his day (three hundred or so years ago) would let their husband know he's their master.

Poor Perrault. He was such an optimist. All a woman has to do to stop her wolfish husband abusing or killing her is to be passive and submissive.

But, if you've lived with an abusive wolf you know the truth.

The truth is the same as it probably has always been. It doesn't matter how passive you are, if he's a wolf in a certain kind of mood – the abuse will happen.

Sadly, so many years after he wrote his optimistic view of modern men, Perrault was wrong.

Men do abuse, attack and kill their wives, partners or ex-partners – much, *much* more often than women abuse or kill theirs.

Bluebeard, as we would recognise him today is – in a literal sense – a serial killer.

But there's more to this tale than grotesque physical violence.

Let's look at it from the point of view of emotional violence.

HE CAN KILL YOUR SPIRIT

A wolf can break your spirit.

His reign of terror – as in Bluebeard's story – is so frightening that you literally curl up and die somewhere inside.

As we've said before, death can be a symbol of among other things, a loss of freedom.

Without freedom of thought or expression, you might as well be a stone statue. Life is not meant to be lived like this.

If this is your story, if Bluebeard is the wolf in your bed , you may well feel numb with fear.

The first step is **Discovering** – and admitting to yourself that this is your story.

Only then can you begin to get your life back.

By now, you already know you'll never please him or be able to make him happy.

You've tried that right?

It hasn't worked.

THE LOCKED ROOM...

The Blue-bearded wolf leaves corpses to rot in his back room.

Let's imagine that the human mind is like a house.

We all have untidy rooms. We leave the bad stuff in there, the bits we haven't got round to unpacking and sorting out.

In the subconscious mind so many things can be locked away and kept from conscious awareness. For example, all the rage and pain from childhood such as:

- The humiliation of wetting yourself at school.
- Being ignored by someone you like.
- The boy who felt a fool when he came too quickly and a girl laughed at him.
- The kiss that went wrong.
- Being teased for wearing glasses, braces, having red hair etc.

Of course these types of things happen to all of us as we grow up. It's part of life.

But if a boy has a misogynistic father, a man who doesn't know how to process his emotions, he'll teach his son to despise women.

These feelings can fester away in that locked room of his and turn nasty.

Instead of growing up, maturing and getting over himself, the Blue-beard wolf will spend the rest of his life avenging these wounds on the women who love him.

He might never have laid a finger on you, but what about the things he says?

- Does he threaten to hurt you or your children or pets?
- Have you ever been afraid, because of the things he says or does - that your partner will do something seriously harmful to you or your children?
- Is he cruel to animals?

IF SO – THESE ARE REAL DANGER SIGNS.

If you've already escaped from this wolf, then you can begin to piece your life together.

But if you're still with him you must seek help from an organisation that deals with issues of domestic abuse.

No one deserves to live in fear.

Your life should be a life you love.

Please get help and keep yourself safe while you do so.

A MODERN DAY STORY OF BLUEBEARD...

Once, not long ago, two people met and fell in love at college.

They were both studying IT and had a good laugh together after lectures.

His name was Lewis and he was a bit weird but also funny and sexy.

Her name was Sophie and she was quiet and shy. They made a great couple – everyone said so.

When they got together properly, he told her he'd had a couple of girlfriends before, but they were bitches and he'd dumped them.

About a year after they started going out, Lewis started to get moody. Sophie did her best to cheer him up.

He hated it if she asked him too many questions about why he was calling her vile names and throwing things about so she kept quiet.

He closed down on her – sometimes for days at a time and she had to tread carefully around him.

On one occasion, he slapped her so hard she fell back and hit her head on the corner of a table.

He didn't mean to do it and he felt awful afterwards. Sophie understood him when he told her that she'd made him do it.

She talked too much apparently.

They got married and slowly Sophie's friends stopped coming round.

Sophie used to escape from Lewis by taking long, hot showers. It was as though she was cold and dead inside.

She thought there might be something wrong with her.

She was always making Lewis angry and most days she couldn't think straight.

One night Sophie was having a lovely shower. Lewis had been weirder than usual lately, but she put that down to pressure at work.

She was towelling off when he came into the room. He smiled at her, grabbed her hair and told that one day, when she was least expecting it, something bad would happen.

Then he banged her head on the tap just so she understood. Then he threw her on the floor and raped her.

Sophie was confused. She didn't know whether it was rape or not. After all, he was her husband and she often had sex without being that into it – especially nowadays.

But all women did that didn't they?

The next morning she went downstairs and Lewis was holding her cat, Jayzee in his arms.

Jayzee was obviously dead.

Lewis, smiling, explained that the cat had been run over. Sophie didn't believe him. They lived in a quiet cul-de-sac and the cat hardly ever left their garden. But she didn't ask questions.

Best not to.

Sophie was shaking with fear for days afterwards. She lost so much weight she started to get weak. She got to thinking that maybe she ought to leave Lewis. But she didn't know if she was strong enough to do that.

She buried the cat in the garden and sat by his grave every day, shivering with fear.

Had the bad thing happened yet? She didn't think so.

She had a horrible feeling Lewis wasn't finished yet.

The End

QUICK WRITE

Grab your notebook and go somewhere peaceful. Somewhere you feel comfortable.

Write about the most traumatic and painful experience of your life with an emotionally abusive man.

Your IWW is right there at your side, sitting quietly by the inner camp fire of your imagination.

She knows what you are ready to write.

She will help you write what is right for your recovery.

She understands your feelings, your thoughts.

She won't allow this experience to bring you any more harm.

What were you feeling when it started?

Did you feel a storm coming?

How did the incident unfold?

What did you think was going on?

Did you try and talk to anyone else about it afterwards.

PART IV
DIOL

"I write entirely to find out what I'm thinking, what I'm looking at, what I see and what it means... what I want and what I fear..." (*Joan Didion*)

CHAPTER 24

WHAT IS DISCOVER, IMAGINE, OBSERVE, LOVE?

What is DIOL?

It's a technique, a series of simple steps in other words it's a method for recovery.

By combining the known therapeutic benefits of writing with certain simple spiritual practises, **DIOL** can help you recover from the trauma of emotional abuse.

It was discovered through careful research and trial and error.

It was forged through experience.

As we've said before, the long-term effects of emotional abuse are deep-seated and often debilitating.

Your ability to function in the world might have been severely impaired by the abuse.

You might have manifested all kinds of nervous anxiety-related symptoms in order to deal with what you have been through.

DIOL aims to help you work through all these things in a subtle, gentle yet powerful way. It does not promise a quick fix. It simply delivers the awareness of your own needs back to you.

It has the gentle power to help you to create your own recovery.

You can use it on its own or as part of a programme of recovery.

If you need medication, especially in the early stages of recovery, that's fine. USE whatever resources you find useful to get well.

A good therapist might encourage your writing practise.

You might want to take along some of what you've written to share with her.

DISCOVER YOUR STORY

Our thoughts stream though our minds like bubbles from a child's plastic wand.

They appear, pop and are gone.

For the most part this is a good thing. The human mind has to have the capacity to forget. Otherwise we'd be carrying the weight of every moment we'd ever lived around with us. It would be a slow kind of death by memory, squeezing all the joy out of life.

We'd be exhausted with every mundane moment, crushed under mountains of minute details.

Social life would be very dull.

We'd have to keep our lives and experiences to the minimum or we'd be overwhelmed.

However, what is much more important than recalling stuff, for instance – the exact number of black ants that traipsed through your kitchen on a Tuesday in July, is the discovery and understanding of what such an event might *mean* to you.

SO, USING THE ANT INVASION EXAMPLE:

- A Buddhist with an attitude of non-violence would be pulling her hair out trying to figure out how to get rid of them without harming a single one.
- A house-proud nurse would be concerned about hygiene – and would probably go out immediately to buy ant powder.
- A young mother would be concerned about using poison –

in case it harmed her child. She might have to use boiling water on the anthill.

- An expert in wildlife might choose to study these interesting little creatures, setting up a series of experiments and write a paper on ant behaviour in the home.
- A wolf might blame his partner for causing the ants to invade his house – because the woman is a slut and doesn't clean the place as she should.
- And someone with a phobia – fear of ants (myrmecophobia) – might have to move house.

THE POINT IS THAT EXPERIENCES ARE ONLY RELEVANT BECAUSE OF their *meaning* in our lives. And what something means to us might not always be obvious – even to ourselves.

We can get used to abusive behaviour until it becomes normal to us.

Especially when the abuse comes from someone we love. By exploring the personal meaning of your story, you'll reclaim your authentic self.

So if someone you love, or have loved - has behaved abusively – the meaning of that behaviour needs to be unravelled.

What does it mean to you personally?

- To be called vile names?
- To be told you are ugly?
- To be forced to have sex when you don't want to?
- To be humiliated in front of your children?
- To lose your career because of your relationship?

Some people won't mind the first one but will be deeply hurt and angry over the last.

Some people will be damaged by sexual coercion, but don't care if their partner thinks they are ugly.

To find out what shape the pattern of your abusive relationship has been is always the first step in recovery.

To find out what you really think, fear and understand you have to catch the thought bubbles before they pop.

To do that - you write.

You do the Quick Writes and the following questionnaire, and then you've got a portfolio of words, ideas, concerns, dreams, nightmares and wishes to work with.

To understand where your relationship went wrong – you have to **Discover** your story.

Once you have that – you have the power to reshape your life.

IMAGINE A NEW ENDING

When the writers of the TV series Star Trek imagined hand-held communication devices they were inspiring the invention of the mobile phone.

When Mary Wollstonecraft (1797-1851) imagined that women might one day have power, not over men, but over themselves; she was inspiring the liberation of women.

There are many games we can play with our subconscious mind. Positive games that help recovery. Playfulness is the realm of this part of our psyche. The imagination takes off on wings if we give it something fun to mess around with.

You can imagine a new way to live your life after the abuse.

Some of us come to a crossroads after we've crawled out of an abusive relationship.

We feel broken, defeated, and damaged. I know this because I've been at this crossroads and the signposts indicated two clear and equally frightening directions:

One – give up. It's over.

Love, life, pleasure are all gone.

Take up full-time drinking, smoking or any other damaging unhealthy pastime to blot out the pain. Sit on sofa for the rest of my days and eat pizza.

Do not go out of front door unless there's a major earth tremor. Order in plenty of booze, cigarettes and pizza. Buy leggings and over-sized t-shirts in bulk. Keep curtains drawn.

Do not hang mirrors on walls or walk in the sunshine or grow flowers or have friends round or write/read books. It's all pointless.

Two – do not give up.

It's just begun.

There is love, life and pleasure to come. Focus on one thing at a time. It'll be really hard and lonely for a while.

There will be sadness so heavy it feels like I'm defeated – but I'm not.

One day at a time. Go out. Work.

Even if it's just a job in a café.

Know that sorrow, anger and fear will not last forever. Somewhere out there – there's a life you love waiting to be imagined.

Ask for help if needed.

Go to the doctor or check in with a women's group set up for people just like you.

You are not alone.

You are stronger than you think. Much stronger.

It's not the falling down that matters – it's the getting up that counts.

Write, write your thought, feelings and stories – imagine and write and keep on writing.

ONE OF THE TECHNIQUES I'VE USED IN ORDER TO GET UP AGAIN – IS imagination.

It's simple and it's free.

Writing is a good way of harnessing its power. Perhaps imagination is the most powerful weapon we each have to defeat our inner demons. Because that - in the end – is what an abusive wolf will do to.

He will set loose inner demons in your head.

He will make you believe you are worthless, mad, weak and stupid.

You are not.

When you've **Discovered** the story he's trapped you in – you make up a new ending.

So easy it seems absurd. How can this make a difference?

Imagination. It sets you free.

As Bob Marley pointed out:

"... emancipate yourself from mental slavery, none but ourselves can free our minds..."

There's an exercise at the end of the questionnaire to help you re-script, re-frame, re-programme, re-imagine the best ending for your story.

The best ending for you that is.

OBSERVE YOUR EMOTIONS AS THEY GROW MORE POSITIVE

"...when your heart speaks, take good notes..."
Judith Campbell

ONCE YOU'VE BEEN IN CONTACT WITH YOUR **INNER WISE WOMAN** and she's helped you **Discover** your story and **Imagine** a new ending to your story – it's a shame to lose contact with her.

She's always there.

Always with you.

She's a part of all of us – an archetype of great courage, clarity and compassion.

Once you've finished this book and are moving forward – buy a new notebook.

Keep it by your bed, or carry it around all the time. You don't have to write in it every day.

But write in it often.

Write what your heart is thinking.

Write what you need to make sense of.

Write about your childhood, your love of swimming and the dream you had last night.

Write your heart out and then see it on the page.

Words make sense of feelings. They give it form. Feelings have a function. Yet we don't really understand what most of them are for.

However, emotions are a part of what drives us and shape our lives. The more you operate with a good understanding of what your feelings are – the more you check in with them; the more you notice something magical.

Your feelings grow more positive.

Of course, it isn't magic. And life is not one big happy chocolate cake all the livelong day.

Life is messy. It's everything. The ups and downs, the agony – the bliss. And everything in between.

But if you give your feelings room to 'just be', by writing them down then for some reason psychologists haven't quite got to grips with yet, you'll have more positive ones.

So, keep a journal, a diary, a notebook, a pillow book, morning pages or evening scribbles – it doesn't matter what you call it.

Write. Write and **Discover**. Write and **Imagine**. Write and **Observe.**

LOVE YOUR LIFE...

"... love the life you live, live the life you love...'
Bob Marley

WHY NOT LOVE LIFE?

If you've escaped your mental captivity – it's perfectly possible. Write down the things you love.

Whatever they are.

Music, reading, dancing, sailing, running, chatting to friends, sitting on the beach, going to the library, playing with your children...

Once you've got used to writing down your feelings and thoughts in a notebook on a regular basis – read it all back every time you finish one of these journals. What has given you a good feeling?

Family?

The natural world?

A warm bath?

Strong coffee?

Being free to watch your favourite films?

NOTICE THESE THINGS.

They are probably very simple.

They don't usually cost a lot of money. They're the smile you get from a friend, the birthday card you write to your daughter on her eighteenth.

Notice how you live your life without the wolf. Notice how you are re-shaping your life and creating your true authentic self.

Now you're free you can make it up as you go along. Of course you'll have bills to pay, bins to take out, and chores around the house but that's all part of it.

The bigger picture is finding the diamonds in the dust.

The little nuggets of pleasure that are there for the taking. Do you like sitting in the garden reading a thriller? Then do it more.

Did you feel guilty if you did it when you were with him?

Hooray, you're free from his abusive form of slavery. Celebrate.

Once you've sorted out the small pleasures, then move onto the bigger ones.

Did you always want to take a course? Get a qualification?

Now is the time.

Think about what you want to do in your life and plan it out in your journal.

Then go out and live it. **Love it.**

What about living in a new town?

Downsizing to a different part of the country? Voluntary service overseas? Write it. Plan it. Think it.

What feelings do you get when you think about these things? Write them. Observe them.

Then go out and shape that life of yours.

It belongs to you. No one can tell you how to live, how to be. Not any more.

Here's a thing. Life itself is the only constant that you can rely on. Apart from taxes and the earth turning.

You might as well fall in love with it - in all its messy, chaotic, exciting beauty.

It's yours now.

Love the life you live – and live it out.

You can't go wrong if you do.

Thanks for a good, solid philosophy of life, Bob.

CHAPTER 25

DISCOVER YOUR STORY – PART ONE: THE QUESTIONNAIRE

How to complete the questionnaire
Which nightmare fairy-tale is yours?
In this section we'll discover what kind of wolf you've had in your bed and which story role he's forced you to play.

The idea is that by understanding who he is, and what story-world he inhabits, you can begin the work of recovery.

You might find that there are several stories and wolf types that apply strongly to you. That's okay. Wolves are often frightening banal.

They share patterns of behaviour – but usually one story will be their favourite.

By discovering the primary attitude of the wolf you loved, you'll be able to get a much better grip on how he has manipulated you.

Then you'll be able to discover which nightmare story he trapped you in, as well as getting a grip on which role he's cast you in. And how he likes to play his part in your nightmare.

We'll take this discovery into the next section and do the real work **which is Imagining** a new ending.

Re-writing the story to make it your own.

How to Respond to the Statements in the Questionnaire:

- Read each question and circle the response that applies most closely to your wolf or your relationship.
- It may well be that all of the statements apply to your wolf but pick only one.
- Choose the one statement that seems to be the truest or most consistent behaviour or character trait.
- Don't spend too long thinking about it.
- Simply use your intuition to find the most likely response.
- Answer each question quickly. Your responses will be more accurate.
- Allow yourself to be open and intuitive as you read each question. One of the side-effects of being with an emotionally abusive man is that your decision-making skills are out of practice, so this is a safe space to work with them.
- Trust your **IWW** to guide you to the right answers.

You do know the truth about him.

You can make good decisions.

You will find the answers you need and the most helpful way of processing all the hurt and pain he has caused you.

Fairy tales are comforting even when they talk about difficult truths. This is because they are tales we tell our children; stories we might know from our own childhood. This gives them a certain distance from the reality of our adult lives, even if they contain the deep truths that have hurt us the most.

If you can, relax and enjoy the process of answering the questions.

When you're done, have a look at the response chart, and work out which wolf you've had in your bed, and which nightmare fairy story he's forced you to live in.

QUESTIONNAIRE

TEST ONE: How other people see him: Part One:

A: Many people see him as an adrenaline junkie; an independent, strong-willed type with a real zest for life.

B: Most people think he is an organised, fair-minded and moral person.

C: Many people see him as a friendly, open-minded and interesting person.

D: Most people believe him to be efficient, intelligent and goal-driven.

E: Most people think of him as supportive and emotionally involved with those he cares about.

F: He is usually seen as an attractive, amusing and charismatic man.

G: Many people find him enigmatic, intense and protective.

TEST ONE: HOW OTHER PEOPLE SEE HIM: PART TWO:

A: His friends find him intriguing and unpredictable.

B: His friends are less intelligent than him, or so he believes.

C: His friends are usually as competitive as he is – yet he surrounds himself with those who can't beat him in the areas he considers most important.

D: He doesn't have many friends, most people find him a bit odd.

E: His friends admire the way he gets involved in important issues.

F: His friends enjoy his company and find him a good laugh.

G: His friends admire him – but they're also a bit scared of him.

TEST TWO: THE WAY HE ACTS WHEN IT'S JUST THE TWO of you:

What he does:

A: He often criticises and belittles you, without talking properly about problems with you or facing up to reality, leaving you to deal with issues alone.

B: He often tells you exactly how to perform simple tasks and what to say to other people.

C: He is grumpy, bored and cynical – and blames you for his dark moods.

D: When he gets low, he rages about everyone who has prevented him from pursuing his dreams.

E: You often catch him out in a lie but dare not confront him with the truth.

F: He is distant, weird and secretive; convinced that he's not enjoying his life as much as he should be.

G: He bullies you and frightens you with his quick temper and threatening behaviour.

HOW HE MAKES YOU FEEL:

A: That you are unlovable and no one else would put up with you.

B: That you are useless and incapable.

C: That you are bad, evil and mad.

D: That your opinions are worthless.

E: That you are thoughtless and cruel.

F: That you are dull and undesirable.

G: That you are lost and do not exist as a whole person.

TEST THREE.1: AT HIS WORST:

WHEN THE WOLF IN HIM COMES OUT HE:

A: Seems to have many different personalities and has become heavily dependent on you to meet all his needs.

B: Will have bad moods, simmering irritation and sulks that can go on for a week or even longer. You are supposed to guess what you've done wrong.

C: Is like living with two distinct and separate people; you never know if he'll be deeply depressed or extremely hostile.

D: Can become jealous and paranoid. May get involved in criminal or addictive activity and may threaten to cause you serious physical harm.

E: Has multiple affairs in his search for the kind of love that he says that you are too selfish to give him.

F: Expects you to tolerate or join him in sexually perverse or addictive behaviour.

G: Is out of control and frightening when he is angry with you or other people. Prone to violent outbursts.

TEST THREE.2: AT HIS WORST HE:
Part Two – Makes you behave badly to please him by:
A: Following unhealthy obsessions. You've lost control and done things you knew were wrong for you. Sometimes you hate yourself.

B: BECOMING MORE DEFENSIVE AND SHY. YOU'RE TIRED MOST OF the time and feel as if you've disappeared into nothing. Sometimes you feel like a nobody.

C: LOSING YOUR SPARK. YOU'VE ALSO LOST MOST OF YOUR FRIENDS. You've isolated yourself so that you can be there when he needs you. Sometimes you feel like you're going mad.

D: TRYING SO HARD TO PLEASE HIM AND GET HIS ATTENTION THAT you neglect yourself. Sometimes you feel like you can't breathe properly, you're suffocated worrying about the relationship and all the things you've done wrong.

E: LYING TO OTHER PEOPLE ABOUT THE STATE OF YOUR relationship. But the more you pretend to be happy, the harder your life seems to become. Sometimes you have panic attacks.

F: Trying to be as attractive as you can and worrying constantly about your body and your looks. Sometimes you feel ugly and useless as a woman.

G: Hoping that you can find the key to the past and go back to how it used to be between you. Sometimes you feel so frightened you don't know how to cope.

TEST FOUR.1: Which fairy story is he acting out the most?

Part One: How you fit the role he's given you:

A: You never seem to be able to convince him that you love him enough.

B: He does not allow you to talk about how angry or upset his bad behaviour makes you feel.

C: His criticism makes you feel like an evil and crazy woman.

D: You feel that his demands and expectations are impossible to fulfil.

E: He's a Jekyll and Hyde personality – sometimes gentle, sometimes scary.

F: He is openly attracted to other women and you know he lies to you.

G: He is so possessive you feel trapped in every part of your life.

TEST FOUR.2: Which fairy story is he acting out the most?

Part Two: He makes you feel as if the world is:

A: A manic place with too much to do and not enough time.

B: An ugly, frightening place full of terrible people.

C: A place where everyone is better, cleverer and more deserving than you.

D: A difficult, painful place – somewhere you will never truly belong.

E: A dying world with so many problems and all you want to do it help others.

F: Full of gorgeous, wonderful women who are better at sex than you.

G: A terrifying place full of horror, pain and suffering.

INTERPRETING THE QUESTIONNAIRE:

Add all the scores for A, then the scores for B and so on.

The highest scoring letters are ones to make a note of.

For example, if you got a mostly 'As', then this will indicate both the kind of wolf you've had in your bed and the story he's trapped you in.

You may find you have two or more stories with the same high score. This is quite usual. A wolf will dip into several characteristic roles for himself and for you to play.

Each individual wolf will have his own way of acting out the wolf types and archetypal story structures. So no single explanation of a wolf type will fit exactly and the same goes for the story types. What you are looking for is:

THE CLOSEST FIT.

If a story seems familiar as a relationship pattern to you in most ways – even if it differs in others – and you get a high score in that category, then that is your story.

The same goes for the wolf personality types.

Your highest scoring wolf might not fit the profile exactly, but if most of the descriptions about him fit – then that is your wolf.

Each wolf will have one story that suits him the most. This will be the closest fit.

If your scores are evenly spread between several types, you have had a very intelligent and restless wolf in your bed, one who's played all sorts of mind games with you to amuse himself. More like a cat with a mouse than a wolf with its prey.

However, you should find one dominant story – the one with the highest number.

If you don't – and there are two or three high scoring stories with same score, read the interpretation of the scores below and pick the one that applies more often.

Whatever your score, make a note of your highest marks and check the interpretations. After that:

- Read all your high-scoring relevant stories.
- Refer back to the Quick Write notes you made after each story.
- Combine your scores with your intuition and ask yourself these questions: Which story structure did he play with me for the longest amount of time? Which story feels right? What wolf behaviour type was more consistent?
- Using the above method, a combination of intuitive writing and the scores on the questionnaire you will **Discover** which wolf and which story you intuitively picked out as yours.
- Remember: The combination of scores from the questionnaire combined with your responses to the Quick Writes will give you the most accurate, rounded picture of your abusive wolf and his favourite story scenario/scenarios.

A BRIEF OVERVIEW TO HELP YOU INTERPRET YOUR SCORES:

HIGH SCORING AS:
Your wolf's most common character side is that of Mr Entitled.

He needs constant entertainment and adoration.

This wolf prefers to put you in the role of Karen in the Red Shoes. You have to perform for him all the time or he becomes angry and/or unhappy.

During your time with this wolf you've lost direction in your own life. This is because everything you do has to be done for him.

His greatest wish is that you will never change, never stop adoring him, and never stop dancing to the tune in his head.

If this is your story you are likely to be physically as well as emotionally exhausted by living in his world.

HIGH SCORING Bs:

This wolf is commonly known as Mr Know-It-All.

In his eyes he is wise beyond his years and the fount of all knowledge in every subject.

If you've achieved anything in your own life, he will be strangely competitive about it – even to the point of making you feel guilty for your successes.

He likes to cast you in the role of Sleeping Beauty.

In this scenario, his idea of the perfect woman is someone who is completely submissive.

He likes you to be quiet while he is talking – he's not good at conversation because he's too busy talking at you instead of with you.

He prefers to be in charge of all aspects of your life.

HIGH SCORING Cs:

Your wolf is the one who smiles as he slices.

Mr Death-by-a- Thousand-Cuts likes nothing better than to wound you with a withering comment just when you need him to be a good friend.

He'll know all your weak points and pick at them until you have little or no confidence left.

Your story is Hans my Hedgehog.

Somehow you know that something is wrong with him but by the time you realise he's emotionally abusive, he's got you in a Stockholm Syndrome stranglehold.

He is the hardest wolf to leave – the one who makes you feel that you really can make your relationship work if only you become a better person.

His abuse is almost impossible to talk about or to recognise.

But it is cruel and damaging nevertheless.

HIGH SCORING DS:

Your wolf is Mr King-of-the-Control-Freaks.

He likes to know everything about you.

There is a suffocating quality to a relationship with this man and his emotional abuse can tip into physical abuse.

You are trapped in the story of The Little Mermaid - overwhelmed by the demands of his world.

Being with him more than any other wolf – is like walking on eggshells.

Bit by bit you'll find you give up everything familiar to you in order to please him.

However, this wolf likes to take talented women, break them and throw them away.

He will make you feel as if you have no voice.

He might be jealous of other men, or leave you for someone else - just when you've lost everything that mattered to you.

HIGH SCORING ES:

Your wolf is Mr Sheep's-Clothing.

On the surface he's a new age, newly feminist, good loving man.

He's got all the right opinions about human rights, animal rights and/or the ecology.

In public at least, he's a great guy.

He'll make sure everyone knows he helps around the house. But he's got so many sharp edges, claws and teeth when you're alone together it's hard to take.

His emotions seem to run your relationship – basically because you keep hurting them and he gets really pissed about it.

Your story with him is Little Red Riding Hood.

It's like you skipped into this relationship full of hope and sunshine. A kind, gentle, open-minded man like him will be incredibly easy to fall in love with.

However, once he's in your bed, watch out.

What big needs he has – all the better to smother you with...

HIGH SCORING FS:

Your wolf is Mr Smooth and if he ever stops flirting for one minute to pay you attention, it's like the sun shining right in your face.

He's a sex god – or so he thinks.

Your story is The Robber Bridegroom because he's the thief of hearts and he's going to keep on counting his trophies – forever.

This wolf may well end up a lonely, porn-addicted old man.

However, in his prime he's all dazzling, smouldering charm.

If you find any of the trophies he keeps of his other women, he'll convince you that he still loves you too.

He'll set women against each other just for the fun of it.

The Robber Bridegroom robs you of your pride.

He takes hearts and puts rings on fingers without thinking about what his actions really mean.

He's a lover not a thinker when it comes to women. His lies will make you weep.

But he's not capable of the love he talks about so your tears won't make any difference to him.

It's his life and he'll do what he wants.

HIGH SCORING GS:

Your wolf is Mr Macho.

He's strong and capable. An alpha male, a silverback gorilla and a man's man.

But he's the kind of macho wolf who doesn't use his superior strength responsibly.

Once he's in your bed, he'll put you in the role of Bluebeard's wife.

He'll play the most intimidating mind games he can think of.

Even if he's never physically violent towards you, his emotional abuse is blunt and frightening.

He might threaten to hurt you or your pets or your children.

In Bluebeard's castle, the woman is never allowed outside the grounds.

She is doomed to stay on Bluebeard's territory, trying to avoid the temptation of the locked room.

The locked room is a symbol of the darkest part of this wolf's mind.

If you ever get a glimpse of it, you'll be sorry – he'll make sure of that.

PART V
FILLING IN YOUR
FAIRY RING

"If you see a fairy ring
In a field of grass,
Very lightly step around,
Tiptoe as you pass;
Last night fairies frolicked there,
And they're sleeping somewhere near."

William Shakespeare

CHAPTER 26
A MAP OF YOU

Filling in your fairy ring to create a map of you
The fairy ring exercise combines the two sides of your brain.

By filling in the Fairy Ring using words - you'll tap into the logical, organised, left-hand side of your brain.

The logical placement of the people, places and all the things that matter the most to you now, today.

This will show you in what areas you are okay, and which areas of your life still need nurturing.

Using the colour-coding system you can identify what your world looks like on a deeper level.

This taps into the more visual, colourful, symbolic world of the imaginative right-hand side of your brain.

It's a powerful springboard for a freewriting exercise about how your world looks right now.

The Fairy Ring is a way of creating a map of how the wolf and his story has influenced the way you live your life today.

How much do you love this life?

Could you love it more?

After this exercise, you'll complete the quick write.

This freewriting exercise taps into your creative, imaginative and feeling mind – your ability to conceptualise.

Afterwards, you can reflect on both exercises and get a rounded picture of where you are right now.

THE FAIRY RING EXERCISE:

Next you will have a deeper look at your own world by using the Fairy Ring diagram on the next page.

Grab red, green and orange pens. Traffic light colours.

Okay, you are now ready to compete the map of your world as it is now.

If you discovered more than one wolf personality and were trapped in more than one story it doesn't matter.

Copy or photocopy the diagram and stick it into your notebook.

You can complete this exercise as many times as you like.

This is your fairy ring. It is your world – not his.

Think about traffic lights:

Red means danger.

Orange means preparing to move on.

Green means you're free of his influence in this aspect of your life and moving forward.

1. First, in the box at the top of the diagram, write the title of the fairy tale you've been trapped in using the traffic light code. If you feel this story is putting you in danger, use a red pen. Orange means you're ready to move on, and green means you've left him and are free of his influence. If you still feel like you're trapped in this story – write it in large capitals. If not, write in the tiniest writing you can.

2. Using the same system write the name of your wolf using the box at the bottom of the page.

3. The wolf and his story remain outside your world.

4. Inside the circle identify and label everything that is important in your life; family, friends, interests, home, sexuality, work, pets etc. Use the traffic code to illustrate

and highlight the way these elements are still affected or not by the relationship with your wolf. For example, if your sexuality is still affected by toxic love, write it in red.

NB If you have two or more high scoring wolf characters and their stories, you can design a fairy ring for each of them separately.

Then consider this:

Which one has the greatest emotional power over you?

Or, you can place all your high-scoring stories outside one circle and see how you were trapped in more than one role.

It's up to you. This is your fairy ring, design it to reflect your world and the impact of it on your life.

If you like, you can also draw little sketches of people, events or things which seem to belong in the circle.

Fairy Ring Diagram:

Title of My Fairy Tale:

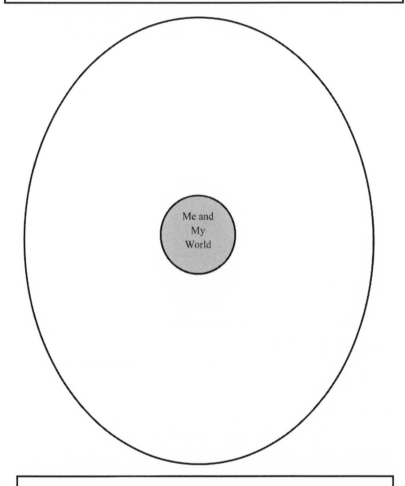

Me and
My
World

Name of my Wolf:

QUICK WRITE

Look at your completed fairy ring and the colour and size that you've identified as the aspects of your world.

Take out your notebook and pen.

Use this prompt:

My world looks like...

Relax. Breathe.

Write the prompt at the top of the page and freewrite using it as a springboard.

Dive into your world.

Be fearless. Write what you feel and think. Let the images come. Let the ideas come and don't stop writing for 5 minutes.

Write about the colours you chose.

Write about people who are in the ring with you.

Write about what is red.

Write about the feeling of orange.

Write about how you got to green.

Write about change. Describe the emotions you feel.

What would your fairy ring look like if it was all green?

Would you have all the same aspects inside?

How do you protect yourself from the wolf world outside the ring?

When you finished writing consider this:

Have you discovered anything that surprises you?

If any other aspects of your life occur to you – add them in.

HOW TO INTERPRET YOUR FAIRY RING:

Have a look at your finished Fairy Ring and the thoughts and feelings you've expressed in the quick write.

If you've done more than one Fairy Ring – which one has the most resonance?

Which feels the closest to your own pain?

Think about your emotional response to this exercise. Did you feel angry, peaceful, sad, powerful, happy whilst making the circle?

Most people feel a mixture of emotions.

I felt both love and sadness when I looked at mine. Love for the people who had stood by me, and sadness for the areas of myself that still needed nurturing.

Are you surprised at the colours you chose for certain aspects of your world?

In the quick write, did anything come to the surface that you weren't expecting?

Is there a difference between the way you wrote the title of the story and the name of your wolf? For example – is the wolf's written in red but the story in green? Or vice versa?

What does this mean to you?

So, now you have **Discovered** your story.

You've designed your Fairy Ring and looked at your world through freewriting.

Do another freewrite to explore this stage of the **DIOL** process if you feel you need to.

BETTER STILL; WRITE A LETTER TO YOUR WOLF, TELLING HIM THAT he is outside your world now.

Explain that you're going to take of yourself from now on and that you will never let anyone harm you by pretending to love you again.

Tell him you are free of him.

Write about freedom, about how good it feels to be rid of him.

Write about your world, the beauty of it.

Tell him he is not allowed to trespass on the land of your world ever again.

It might appear to be quite chaotic at the moment. You've got a collection of freewrites, your notebook, the fairy ring diagrams, lists and letters - but this is the key to the next step in your journey.

Your journey has a way to go yet. You've got the tools you need to set your own world in order, and write your way home to your Self.

This is the most exciting journey of your life.

It's time to start living your own life – a life you love.

Now, in order to get there as quickly and safely as we can - we'll **Imagine** a new ending to your story.

CHAPTER 27
IMAGINE A NEW ENDING

"When patterns are broken, new worlds emerge..." *(Tuli Kupferberg)*

WHAT GOOD DOES IMPINGING A NEW ENDING DO?

After all, the relationship ended the way it did – and abusive relationships always end badly.

Or they just go on getting worse. This is because the abuse cycles get shorter. What that means is that you get less and less of the nice wolf – and more of the abusive one.

If you are still living with a wolf, now you've figured him out – are you sure he can change?

Possibly.

Although why would he?

Research shows that abusive men are not born they are made. From his early years an abusive man will have learned that women are there to give men sexual pleasure.

Power over women is not something a wolf gives up easily. It's intoxicating.

REMEMBER: AN UNREFORMED WOLF DOES NOT KNOW HOW TO LOVE.

Your decision to stay with him is up to you.

But you can still rewrite the ending of your story.

Rewriting the script opens your mind to new possibilities. It gets your imagination working on different ideas of how the future might turn out.

Imagination is the most underused resource of the human mind. Within its landscape impossible things roam free. If you choose to make use of it you are accessing the largest part of your brain. Not in the physical sense.

But in the sense that imagination has no boundaries.

Use it for good, for healing and for the creation of truth, beauty and love in your life.

Then you will set yourself free.

By playing creatively with your unspoken wishes, dreams and desires you take back the power you gave away.

This work takes time. Maybe you think you don't have an imagination.

You do.

But it may need reawakening.

As children we know instinctively how to access this part of ourselves. Many of us forget how to get there once we're grown, except in our sleep.

An easy route back to the rich soil of your imagination is through writing.

Writing a new ending for your story is like a wish-fulfilling jewel.

It has the same cycle of growth as a new-born child.

- You give birth to it by writing it down.
- It grows and develops with your loving, nurturing presence.
- Finally, it matures and you come to this new land – your life after wolf.

REMEMBER: *NO ONE BUT YOURSELF CAN FREE YOUR MIND.*

And the only tools you need are a notebook, a pen and an open mind.

Thinking, dreaming and reflecting are just as important as the actions you take in your everyday life.

Work, childcare and household chores matter too. But sometimes it's too easy to accept a life of emotional abuse and its effects on your psychology because you're too busy.

Ease up.

Take some time out.

This step won't take long.

In fact, it won't take any longer than it would take to read a magazine. Or chat to a friend on the phone. Or watch a gripping drama on TV.

Probably less time than these activities.

Everything works in cycles. The seasons in nature. The seasons of your life.

And there is a lifecycle to all relationships.

A healthy, loving relationship has inner cycles and yet the relationship simply expands. Good love grows and blooms and changes in quality over the years.

It has the hallmark of being self-sustaining and supportive for both of you.

The lifecycle of everything in nature and beyond is structured like a story.

A journey is taken.

It has a beginning, a middle and an end.

Morning, afternoon, night.

Birth, love, death.

An unhealthy relationship doesn't end with the break-up. It ends when you are truly free of him.

In between his abuse he lets you rest, and you've felt love and gratitude for that. You've been manipulated into loving a man who did not deserve to be loved.

Now it's time to change all that. Write a new ending. Take your power back.

QUICK WRITE

In your notebook, have a look at the page where you designed your Fairy Ring.

What fairy story or stories did you **Discover** you were trapped inside?

Think about your story.

How does the underlying structure of your life mirror the fairy tale?

What are the symbols that resonate with you the most?

What happened in the end?

Give your **Imagination** permission to play on the page.

Use this prompt to begin your freewrite:

At last she discovered a way out and she....

What did she do?

Turn him into a bat?

Run off with all his treasure?

Grow back her feet and run away?

Find a hidden door in Granny's house and run away?

Push him down a well?

Wake up, walk out and take a degree in business studies?

Grow a fishtail and swim back to her own world?

Allow your imagination to take flight.

Go crazy. No one need ever read what you've written. Allow your IWW to guide your hand.

Some of your thoughts might be dark and vengeful. Getting them out on the page is safe.

You can face your inner darkness and accept it on the page.

A passionate anger does not make you a bad person. It's normal to feel like this is if you've been abused. By recognising this part of yourself, these feelings are less likely to be acted out in the real world.

Let your IWW advise you.

She will not show you anything in your own mind that you can't handle.

She will let you know if you need to talk to a therapist or someone else about your feelings and thoughts.

Accept yourself as you are.

We are all a mixture of light and shade.

Have a light touch and an open heart.

If you like, you can end this exercise by writing a wish list with the title:

My List of Dreams, Goals and Desires for the coming year are:

EXAMPLE OF HOW TO CREATE A NEW ENDING BASED ON THE Red Shoes.

THINKING ABOUT THE STORY:

Read your story chapter again.

Make notes if you need to. Look at your fairy ring page in your notebook.

Can you see ways in which the wolf in your bed has stifled your career?

Do you feel worn out by your efforts to please him?

Have you paid less attention to your physical looks because your whole life is out of control?

Have you lost your self-confidence?

How might you take care of yourself if you're burned out and exhausted after spending so long trying to please this wolf?

If the Red Shoes fit, find a way to take them off.

IMAGINING THE NEW ENDING...

In your notebook write a new ending to the story.

All that matter is that in your version, Karen's story ends well for her.

How might Karen get rid of her shoes without cutting off her feet?

Maybe she gets hold of some magic shoe polish and takes back control of her feet.

Or perhaps her feet grow back and she runs barefoot back home to her adoring guardian, the old woman – her IWW.

What punishment might an angel of the goddess mete out to *him*?

Perhaps the wolf/soldier is forced to dance alone forever, with no one to admire him or amuse him.

Where does Karen go once she is free?

Perhaps she takes the next train out of the village and sets up a successful dancing academy in the city.

How long should I spend on this?

Spend about ten to fifteen minutes on this – let yourself go – let this new story spill out through your pen.

Of course you can spend longer if you like.

Or it might only take you five minutes. Whatever.

This is a very powerful exercise.

You've opened the door to the rest of your life.

Observe your feelings as they Grow more Positive

"A traveller without observation is a bird without wings." *Sa'di*

Feelings never last.

They are like the tides. They ebb and flow.

What seems overwhelming one day is only a slight ache the next. Can you name your feelings?

This is harder than you think. But the more you observe them – the more quickly feelings pass through you.

They rise and fall. They have somewhere to go.

All they want is that you notice them. Then they've done their job. They're gone.

Too often we don't deal with our feelings because we don't know what they are.

We let them torment us. Or we try to ignore them. That's when they cause real problems.

If you find yourself acting out a difficult emotion, without knowing why you feel so bad – you're in trouble.

If you can give your feelings a name – you give them a home. They belong to you.

There are hundreds perhaps thousands of subtly different states of feeling. They are a barometer of the heart.

If the weather is stormy inside you, that's how it'll be all around you. By naming a feeling not only do you give it a home, but more importantly, you set it free.

A feeling you've acknowledged has done its job. It's let you know what's going on in deep inside the powerhouse of you. Heart and soul.

Feelings are always just passing through.

BY OBSERVING YOUR FEELINGS YOU – SET THEM FREE.

Also, you know whether to ask for help. If a series of very low feelings are present most of the time, you might be suffering from clinical depression.

There's no shame in that. Go to the doctor and ask for help. That's what feelings are for – they give you insight.

Inner Sight.

Your Inner Wise Woman knows what you are feeling and why.

She's always there, rootling about in the flames of your soul looking for good feelings to dish up to you.

But only once you've accepted the bad ones, the hurt ones, the low ones.

All feelings are part of you and everyone has the same capacity for them.

WOLF MEN OF THE EMOTIONALLY ABUSIVE CLAN HAVE WALKED AWAY from theirs.

This doesn't mean they don't have them. Emotions which are ignored fester like gangrene. They turn bad.

Let him deal with his stuff.

You only have a responsibility to deal with yours.

You have the power and the right to own your emotions. All of them.

You can name them, accept them and watch them pass.

For some reason that is not quite understood yet – by doing this you will discover more positive emotions emerging.

Exciting isn't it?

The key to greater happiness is careful observation of something that you already have.

Watching your feelings is like watching birds or clouds. It's an observation of something natural.

There's nothing self-centred or weird about doing this. It's your gift at birth as a human being.

Your right to come into full self-knowledge and self-love.

Once you've trained yourself to this simple task, your compassion will grow. You'll have more to give the people around you who deserve your love. That's how it works. An alchemy of the soul.

Sit in a comfortable position.

Take a few deep breaths.

Close your eyes, put one hand over your heart.

Tune into how you're feeling right now.

Name that emotion!

HERE'S A LIST OF A FEW EMOTIONS TO GET YOU STARTED. READ through both lists before you start:

Good Feelings:

Open type: understanding, kind, accepting, sympathetic, interested, free, amazed, easy, confident, receptive, satisfied, relaxed.

Happy type: joy, elation, glad, festive, grateful, delighted, lucky, sunny, merry, jolly, giggly, playful, charming, surprised, blissful, blithe, cheerful.

Alive type: courageous, energetic, sense of wonder, frisky, optimistic, liberated, free, thrilled, spirited, animated, bright, bubbly, lively, exuberant, excited.

Content type: tranquil, calm, blessed, quiet, certain, serene, easy, encouraged, reassured, peaceful, comfortable, pleased, certain, chilled, composed, unruffled, placid, undisturbed, imperturbable.

Love type: loving, affectionate, tender, devoted, caring, attracted, passionate, admiration, considerate, warm, touched, drawn toward, loved, close, intimate, comforted, sympathy, connected, empathy.

Interested type: fascinated, inquisitive, curious, engrossed, intrigued, focussed, concerned, puzzled, enquiring, questioning.

Positive type: eager, enthusiastic, excited, intent, keen, earnest, inspired, determined, motivated, stimulated, electric, bold, hopeful, confident, brave, daring, optimistic, daring, challenged, re-enforced.

Strong type: impulsive, dynamic, unique, hardy, stoic, free, certain, tenacious, protective, balanced, secure, safe.

Difficult Feelings:

Angry type: irritated, fuming, hostile, provoked, cross, boiling, offensive, resentful, infuriated, enraged, annoyed, upset, hateful, bitter, aggressive, inflamed, incensed, indignant, hateful, unpleasant.

Depressed type: low, sulky, despairing, disgusting, miserable, guilty, discouraged, dissatisfied, disappointed, ashamed, detestable, despicable, terrible, lost, empty, repulsive, powerless, meaningless, grey, melancholy, dejected, weighed, gloomy, pessimistic.

Confused type: tense, upset, unsure, uneasy, pessimistic, unsure, uneasy, doubtful, perplexed, hesitant, disillusioned, distrustful, uncertain, stupefied, misgivings, perplexed, embarrassed, sceptical.

Helpless type: lonely, dominated, exhausted, useless, forced, despairing, distressed, woeful, tragic, pathetic, incapable, unconfident, paralysed, inferior, frustrated, incapable, hesitant.

Indifferent type: insensitive, blank, dull, nonchalant, reserved, weary, bored, cold, disinterested, lifeless, numb, disdainful.

Afraid type: apprehensive, fearful, terrified, suspicious, wary, menaced, quaking, cowardly, threatened, anxious, alarmed, panic, nervous, scared, worried, frightened, timid, shaky, restless, doubtful, alarmed.

Hurt type: crushed, tormented, alienated, deprived, wronged, humiliated, pained, tortured, rejected, offended, heartbroken, agonised, appalled, dejected, injured, aching, victimised, sick, afflicted, damaged, wounded, distressed.

Sad type: tearful, dismayed, sorrowful, pained, grief, anguish, desolate, mournful, grieved, lonely, unhappy, desperate, pessimistic, downcast, low, gloomy

QUICK WRITE

Grab your notebook, a pen and your favourite hot drink.

Make a list of three positive emotions from the list above.

Explore each emotion by using this prompt:

What is (positive emotion)?

Freewrite on each emotion for 5 minutes.

You may find memories coming to the surface such as: jokes, family outings, moments of great peace etc.

Notice how your mind puts these emotions into words.

You are combining your rational, thinking mind with your feeling, soulful mind. Good.

Next, pick three negative emotions.

Explore in the same way.

What is (negative emotion)?

It isn't harmful to recognise the truth about how you feel.

By writing these things you *will not* bring them back into your life.

Quite the opposite. You are exposing them to the light. This sets them on their way.

Be fearless. Your IWW will only let you write what you can deal with right now.

The light of consciousness will make you whole.

Through the alchemy of brilliant awareness your negative emotions will be refined.

Remember: Turn your wounds into words and turn your words into wisdom.

By understanding your own wounds – you will become a more compassionate person.

This means you have more to offer other people.

You'll also have a greater depth of understanding in all situations whether it's work or home related.

Your Story

By now you might feel ready to write the whole story of your love affair with your wolf.

It doesn't have to be a novel-length work of great fiction. A few pages might cover it.

Look on it as a journey, a quest to save yourself.

In the beginning - you met him and fell in love.

Describe the circumstances of your meeting. How did he seduce you? What did it feel like?

In the middle – you encountered obstacles in your relationship.

What were the main two or three turning points in the love affair?

How did he build up the abuse?

What incidents made you realise he was in control of your life?

In the end – you were left with two choices. To stay in love with him or to move on. This is a great scene.

Write down all the brilliant things you'd say to him if you'd thought of them at the time.

This is creative non-fiction. You don't have to be completely accurate!

Make the story yours.

Take back your power.

Your Notebook

... is your friend for life.

Keep on writing.

Whenever you need to work something through or you can't sleep or a big change is going on in your life.

Write your heart out.

Through good times as well as bad. Look out for lovely notebooks at cheap prices. They are everywhere.

The next notebook you buy can be a diary, a journal, five-year diary, or a pillow book.

Call it what you like, it will never let you down.

In your notebooks over the years you will find the closest friend you'll ever have.

Your IWW is always with you.

She knows you better than anyone.

You can rant, enthuse, puzzle, wax lyrical, crack jokes, and cry with joy on the page.

You can write about a holiday, a child being born, a new job or a rainy day.

THE PEN IS MIGHTY

The pen is mightier than the sword because it has a magic power. Yes. The pen in your hand is a direct line to your creative imagination.

The power of imagination is a bit like magic.

It's otherworldly and a bit mystical. It can transform things. It can turn wolves into thin air.

It contains the power of true courage. Actually, it isn't magic at all.

It's just you – but on the inside.

If you are in regular contact with your inner self, your IWW, the part of you that is truly balanced and loving and takes your health and wellbeing seriously – you are in control of your life.

The pen will give you the strength to recover.

The strength to deal with whatever life throw at you – good and bad.

Also, the pen is cheap.

Available in all supermarkets and stationary outlets.

It sits neatly inside a handbag.

No one can stop you taking up your pen and writing what you think and what you feel in your own damn notebook.

So. Here's the way to go beyond this book.

Harness the force of **Observation**.

It will keep you healthy and help you find your own path through the forest we call life:

- Keep on writing about your *emotions* in your notebook.
- Keep on writing about your *thoughts about your emotions*. Ask yourself – what do I think about how I'm feeling right now? The answer will give you insight. Insight will give you courage, compassion, clarity.
- Explore all the emotions in the emotion list. Watch as they pass through you. Express them on the page through your mighty pen. Notice how they grow more positive. By paying attention to your true feelings, you'll become more aware of the frequent positive emotions you're experiencing. A quiet sense of peace is a positive emotion. Don't miss it. Observe it. A new interest in a subject – catch that curiosity and recognise its goodness. A comfortable feeling as you listen to your favourite music. Observe your feelings – all of them. And the good ones will show up more often.
- Don't forget that life is always a mix of light and shade. There will be new obstacles at every stage of your life. Don't dismiss negative emotions. Name them and observe as they pass through. As the Buddhists say, it's like watching clouds blowing across a clear blue sky. Nothing stays the same. Sadness passes. Anger recedes. It's okay to feel what you feel. Your feelings have been discounted for too long. It's time for you to honour them again.

KEEPING A PEN HANDY WILL KEEP YOU HEALTHY.

The mighty pen will keep you strong.

Wow! Your writing can save you.

You don't have to sign up to a religion you're not sure of or join a cult or practise for long hours every day.

Just pick up the pen whenever you want to.

The simplest method is often the most effective.

CHAPTER 28
LOVE THE LIFE YOU LIVE...
... AND LIVE THE LIFE YOU LOVE.

"...I believe that what all of us are really searching for is this divine essence within ourselves. When we are far away from our Higher Self, we feel what Roberto Assagioli has so aptly called 'Divine Homesickness'..."
Susan Jeffers

THE KEYS TO LOVING YOUR LIFE...

Firstly, you have to keep the wolf from your door.

Not only the real wolf, the abusive man – but also the wolf of financial ruin that so often accompanies women after a break-up.

So, you've got to sort out the practical and the emotional.

Secondly, you'll have time to consider what kind of life you love.

And thirdly – what about loving again?

Hmm. It helps if you know how to spot a wolf early.

KEEPING THE WOLF FROM YOUR DOOR...

The first part of this book was a Wolf Recovery Kit.

Once you've **Discovered** your Story, **Imagined** a New Ending and learned how to **Observe** your Feelings as they Grow more Positive – where do you go?

Into the next stage of your life.

ANY TRAUMATIC EXPERIENCE – WHETHER IT'S A CAR ACCIDENT, A fire in the home or living with an abusive man - will change who you are.

It's okay to change. The person who comes out of the wreckage of an abusive relationship and works on her recovery is very likely to be a more compassionate, clear-thinking and courageous person than she was before.

This is your gift to you and the world. Accept it with gratitude.

Okay. Now for the practical stuff.

QUICK WRITE

Grab your mighty pen and beloved notebook and write this question at the top of a new page:

What practical details do I need to deal with right now?

Make a list of everything you need to sort out. Finances, work, health, home, rent, mortgage, divorce, study, children, pets etc.

Look back over your list when you've finished. What is in your control?

What do you need help with? Who can you ask for help?

How does this list make you feel?

If you're overwhelmed, then write about that feeling.

When you've finished that – get on with dealing with the things you can deal with. Ask for help from the people who can help.

Take one small thing at a time. Make a phone call. See the doctor. One thing at a time is how it works.

And as much as you can – try not to involve your wolf in your personal decisions.

MOVING ON

Are you still in contact with your wolf?

If you've just left the relationship it might be hard to let go. Ask yourself these questions:

- Do you visit him late at night uninvited?
- Do you hide how much contact you're having with him from your friends and family?
- Do you still feel as if he is the only friend you have left and you have no one else to talk to?
- Do you still love him?
- Do you still believe your relationship could work?
- Do you miss the life you had with him even if it was hard?
- Do you phone when you're in trouble?
- Do you miss the future you thought you'd share with him?

ALL THE ABOVE ARE PERFECTLY NORMAL.

An emotionally abusive man will have an incredibly strong hold over you.

He has induced traumatic bonded – tainted love in you.

It's not your fault.

You didn't make him the way he is.

And you didn't do anything wrong by falling in love with him.

Wolves are attracted to women for various reasons.

They love a challenge.

Sometimes they go for strong, sensual women.

They also like to go for women who are vulnerable – say, just after a break-up with family or a previous lover.

None of this is important.

What is important is to keep on writing. Short, sweet bursts focusing on your own recovery and the people in your life who are worth loving:

If you feel guilty – write about guilt.

If you miss him – write about loss and grieving.

If you want to talk to him – write a letter to him in your notebook.

If you call him on the phone – write down how you feel about this later.

If you still love him – write about love.

If you miss the past – write about the good times.

If you regret the past – write about the pain.

If you are afraid of the future – write about that.

If you still wish or believe that the relationship could work – explore that issue by writing about it.

HOW LONG DOES IT TAKE...

... to get over an emotionally abusive relationship?

WELL, IT DEPENDS ON THE TYPE OF ABUSE AND HOW LONG IT WENT on for.

Moving on means that your wounds become scars.

And the scars eventually fade. This is okay.

We are all scarred by life in some way or another. To deny that is to deny what it is to be human. Embrace it all.

Life.

The whole messy, chaotic, crazy, blissful, heart-breaking, great big beautiful whirl of it.

On average I suppose, it should take about two years to recover from an abusive relationship.

WHEN I SAY RECOVER, I MEAN TO BE OVER IT ENOUGH TO function. To be over it enough to **Observe** your Positive Feelings Growing more Frequent.

To plan and start **Loving** your Life.

That's okay isn't it?

You can do it.

And the journey is amazing. It's difficult and funny and sad and irritating and weird.

But it's doable.

After one year, you'll have taken back control of the practical details of your life.

And after two years, the scars are beginning to fade.

Especially if you've turned your wounds into words – and your words into wisdom.

If you never allow yourself to address the deeply painful issues of emotional abuse, you might well suffer a sort of low-grade grieving process for years and years.

Even if this is the case – even if you ended the abusive relationship twenty or thirty or more years ago – you can still use the **DIOL** method to recover.

You can free your mind and soul with a pen and notebook and a willingness to explore the dark corners of your heart.

Check in with your IWW.

She's always there.

She always has been.

She's the best part of you.

DISCOVER WHAT KIND OF LIFE YOU LOVE... AND THEN LIVE IT

This is actually a spiritual choice.

To **Love the Life you Live**, you have to be present.

Remember the Little Mermaid?

She left her element and her home just to go into the world of her prince. There she felt pain with every step. That's not how life should be.

Sure, there will be the usual stuff to deal with. Grumpy relatives, scratchy shop assistants, awkward bosses and so on.

There is sickness, ageing and death. It comes to all of us. It's impossible to be happy, serene, patient and caring every moment of every day.

Yet it is possible to live a meaningful, deeply satisfying life every single day.

Take responsibility for the things which are yours. Be accountable for your shortcomings.

Accept yourself as a normal, fallible human creature.

A realistic approach to life does not mean we can't be spiritual.

Quite the opposite. To **love the life you live** you must choose it.

And it must embrace all of who you are.

You don't have to pretend that you have achieved complete happiness and utter inner peace.

Only a very, very few beings have ever achieved this.

Even the Dalai Lama admits to feeling a bit miffed on occasion.

Loving the Life you Live is about living authentically.

QUICK WRITE

Take up your pen of truth and sit comfortably.

This exercise shouldn't take longer than five minutes.

A human being is a person who does things. She creates. She works. She contributes.

If you could create, work and contribute in a way you loved – what would it look like?

Let's explore this.

Write this question along the top of the page:

What do I Love doing?

Freewrite for 5 minutes.

Read back what you've written.

Have you focussed on career issues or hobbies?

Is it all about gaining or giving comfort and material things?

Have you imagined the impossible?

How can you make your ideas become real?

Do you need to take a course?

Move to a new town?

Apply for a new job?

Are you already doing something – but with a little help you could make it into a business?

Is it possible to take a year out to volunteer in a developing country?

Consider everything you've written about.

Take yourself seriously.

How could you change your life to make it fit what you're good at?

What is stopping you from changing?

Is there anyone positive who might support you in your dreams?

Living is always for real. It's about truly feeling alive. If you feel alive – you're comfortable in your own skin as the French would say.

Getting this feeling is all about finding your way home – curing Divine Homesickness.

Your Inner Wise Woman is your higher self.

Find her cottage in the woods of your subconscious mind and you are home.

And once you know what you really want to do for work, go after it. Make the choice. Ask for help.

How to Spot a Wolf Early

Okay, so you're feeling better and you meet a man... are there any signs or indications that he might be emotionally abusive?

Yes there are.

Take care to read the list below, and check it when you start dating again.

Try not to fall in love before you've done this.

Although remember that some wolves are well hidden. Keep your boundaries strong and listen to your intuition. We often repeat patterns until we've really learned a lesson we need to get the hang of.

Don't give yourself a hard time if you've loved more than one wolf. Remember, a lot of them are single... for reason which are obvious.

Believe that one day you'll find someone who loves you for who you are. Someone who will share your wish to grow emotionally and spiritually into your later years.

THESE ARE THE MAIN WOLF DANGER SIGNS:

- Listen carefully to the things he says. Take even more notice of the things he does. Do they match up? Does he say he loves you very early on in the relationship? Does he act in unloving ways even though he speaks the words of love? **If his actions don't match his words – watch out.**
- Does he **use foul or degrading language when he mentions his ex?** If he does, then the chances are that this is how he'll talk about you when he's discarded you.
- Are there any previous girlfriends of his that you know? Do they say he abused them? Most women do not make up stories of abuse to smear an ex-boyfriend. **If an ex-partner says he's been verbally, physically or psychologically abusive towards her – the chances are that she's telling the truth and he's a wolf.**
- Remember – he might be very skilled at hiding his abusive

LEARN AS MUCH AS YOU CAN ABOUT ADULT ATTACHMENT THEORY.

The ways we connect with other people are often a result of habit.

Watch out for subtle signs of wolfishness that he can't hide – especially at the beginning of a relationship.

The most obvious one of these is this:

He's excessively charming, loving, devoted and giving – and **the relationship becomes very intense very quickly**.

Has he put you on a pedestal right from the start?

This is a very dangerous place to be – even if it feels great to begin with.

Don't try and be perfect.

Be natural in front of him as much as possible – be the way you are with your closest friends. **Allow him to see your imperfections and if he makes sarcastic or unkind comments about your behaviour, values and attitudes – he's a wolf.**

Is he incredibly determined to make you his girlfriend very quickly?

If you need to take time to get to know him, does he back off or not? He should. Love takes time. Let it grow organically. Whirlwind romances are often an indication of problems later on.

If you need some space – does he let you have it?

Love is a delicate flower. It needs time to grow.

If he wants the relationship to be too serious too quickly and gets pissed off if you try to slow it down– it's a red flag.

Does he want to spend all his free time with you straight away?

Of course, you want to get to know each other.

However, it's best to stick to agreed times and activities at first.

Does he 'surprise you' at work or other times when you weren't expecting him?

Does he ignore your requests for clear boundaries?

This is a sign that he's taking control of your life.

Is he showing signs of jealousy early on? **Does he accuse you of seeing other men or flirting - before you're even a proper couple**?

This is a red flag.

Does he think it's okay to make sexist jokes or 'ironic' comments that degrade women?

Even if he's joking, pay attention to how these comments make you feel.

If you are uncomfortable, it's a red flag.

DOES HE **RIDICULE YOUR FRIENDS/FAMILY OR TRY AND CUT THEM out?** If so, this is a red flag.

A new partner should want to fit into your life and get to know the people you care about.

ABOVE ALL, LISTEN CAREFULLY TO YOUR INTUITION, your IWW.

Always pay attention to how a potential new partner makes you feel about yourself and about others.

Write your way through this stage of your new life.

Write about the things he says and what he does.

Write about how you feel and what you think about what you feel.

CHAPTER 29
REAL LOVE... AND HOW TO RECOGNISE IT

R eal love is about connection. It's authentic. It has friendship, tenderness, authentic romance, sex, personal boundaries, healthy communication, and friendship.

It's not the fuss and fandango of fake romantic gestures.

It isn't whimsy and false soppiness.

It's real and deep and wonderful.

It's in the details.

It's about being thoughtful, compassionate and intimate.

It's about knowing when to give the other person space and when to be close.

It takes time to mature. And it gets better over time. It grows with you and it allows you both the space to be exactly who you are without judgement.

For a woman who has suffered the trauma of an emotionally abusive relationship — it is best to approach a new love affair very slowly indeed.

Good things can be stressful as well as bad.

Falling in love can feel a bit like madness.

Take care.

Be thoughtful, compassionate and a good friend to yourself.

TALK TO YOUR FRIENDS AND FAMILY ABOUT HOW YOU ARE FEELING. Allow them to voice any concerns.

Try not to get carried away by a man who is excessively attentive and seductive.

These behaviours are danger signs.

Okay, so he might just be an over-excitable character and not abusive. And if he is, then he should back off with respect if and when you ask him to.

Try to make sure you've dealt with any issues left over from your abusive relationship before you go into a new one.

If you developed any addiction problems – have you sought help?

If you've suffered sexual abuse – you need to take that part of the new relationship very slowly indeed.

With a new lover you should feel excited, respected, joyful, beautiful, comfortable, and safe – all at the same time.

QUICK WRITE

Take out your notebook and pen and settle into a quiet place.

Think of Red Riding Hood skipping through the woods.

How might she have spotted a wolf?

Write this question at the top of the page.

What are the danger signs I'll look out for in a man?

Freewrite for 5 minutes.

Read back what you've written.

Refer back to the list of warning signs.

Have you left any out from the list?

What is your IWW saying to you?

Remember to review the list when you start dating again.

Now, on a new page, write this question:

What do I want from a new partner?

Freewrite for 5 minutes.

Every now and again you can repeat this exercise – or any of the others in this book.

Watch how your thoughts and feelings change over time.

What you will look for in a man now might be different in a year's time.

Do this exercise whenever you need to.

LAST THOUGHTS:

"Eventually we might find that all emotions, all human activities and all spheres of life have deep roots in the mysteries of the soul and therefore are holy." (*Thomas Moore.*)

TO ALL OF YOU HAVE COME THROUGH AN ABUSIVE RELATIONSHIP AND have done the work in this book – my thoughts are with you.

We will probably never meet but you are important to me.

We might be very different people, but on one level we are the same.

We are not victims, we are simply experienced.

Our experiences have been traumatic.

But we are prepared to work on our recovery.

Our souls have been violated but we know we can heal them through self-care.

We are not prepared to let our pain overwhelm us.

Stay strong. Own your story. It has made you more compassionate. And you were always that way.

It's not a crime to fall in love with someone you shouldn't have fallen in love with.

REMEMBER THE MIGHTY PEN AND THE NOBLE NOTEBOOK.

Have them with you wherever you go.

They are like magic talismans in the struggle to love the life you live and live the life you love.

Looking at the situation of emotional abuse from a long way off –

you can see that it's true that those who seemed to be the losers – us – are the winners.

We have heart.

We have the capacity to love.

We know how to feel.

This is what being alive is.

My one great hope is that one day men will not use emotionally abusive tactics to have power and control over women.

And for now, let us spare a thought for those lonely old wolves.

Ask yourself this: How will he end up if women become wise to his tricks?

Ah, now there's a thought.

"...SO THERE HE SITS STILL BY HIS WINDOW, - IF YOU COULD ONLY SEE HIM as you may some day, - weeping more bitterly than ever.

And his white hair has bound him to the stones, and the river of his tears runs away to the great sea..."

From the fairy tale: Tattercoats (English fairy tale: Wordsworth Classics).

RESOURCES

Further Reading:

Psychological and emotional abuse:

Lundy Bancroft, *'Why Does He Do That? Inside the minds of angry and controlling men.'* Berkley Publishing Group; Reprint edition, 2003.

Albert J. Bernstein, Ph. D., *"Emotional Vampires, Dealing with People Who Drain You Dry"*, McGraw Hill, New York, 2001.

Meg Kennedy Dugan & Roger R. Hock, *"It's My Life Now, Starting over after an Abusive relationship or Domestic Violence"*. Routledge, Oxon, 2006.

Writing & journalling inspiration:

Julia Cameron, *"The Artist's Way – A Course in Discovering and Recovering your Creative Self"*, Pan Books, London, 1995.

Louise DeSalvo, *"Writing as a Way of Healing – How Telling our Stories Transforms our Lives"*, Beacon Press, Boston, 1999.

Natalie Goldberg, *"Writing Down the Bones – Freeing the Writer Within"*, Shambhala, Boston & London, 1986.

Susan Jeffers, *"Feel the Fear and do it anyway"*, Random House, Reading, 1987.

Rebecca McClanahan, *"Write your Heart Out – Exploring and Expressing What Matters to You"*, Walking Stick Press, Ohio, 2001.

Thomas Moore, *"Care of the Soul – How to add Depth and Meaning to your Everyday Life"*, Piatk

Tristine Rainer, *"The New Diary – How to use a Journal for Self- Guidance and Expanded Creativity"*, Penguin, USA, 2004.

Books about fairy tales:
 Angela Carter, *"The Bloody Chamber"*, Vintage, London, 1979.
 Maria Tatar, *"The Classic Fairy Tales"*. Norton Press, USA, 1999.
 Catherine Ornstein, *'Little Red Riding Hood Uncloaked: Sex, morality and the Evolution of a Fairy Tale'*, Basic Books, New York, 2002.
 Marina Warner, *"From the Beast to the Blonde"*, Vintage, Wiltshire, 1995.

When you're ready to start dating again:

Ken Page, *"Deeper Dating: How to drop the games of seduction and discover the power of intimacy"*, Shambala, 2015.

Useful Websites (UK)

*www.**womensaid**.org.uk*

*www.**refuge**.org.uk*

www.rspca.org.uk/allaboutanimals/helpandadvice/petretreat

Useful Websites (USA)

www.now.org - National Organization for Women

www.thehotline.org - National domestic violence hotline

Useful Websites (Australia)

www.dvrcv.org.au

www.wesnet.org.au

ABOUT THE AUTHOR

Jill Harris lives in the New Forest in England and writes novels as well as non-fiction.

She loves to hear from readers, and you can email her at jillharris-books@gmail.com

If you'd like to know more about (or receive an advance copy of) Jill's new book, follow this link to subscribe to her newsletter:

http://eepurl.com/dnalCv

Made in the USA
Coppell, TX
30 October 2019